Advance praise for *The P...*

"Motherhood in America *is* a paradox—sentimentalized and devalued at once. The 'natural mothers' Bobel researched show us not just their particular resolutions of the paradox, but also clarify the larger problems of mothering in this difficult world. Bobel has made a wonderful contribution to our understanding of American motherhood in all its forms."

—Barbara Katz Rothman, Professor of Sociology,
CUNY, and author of *Recreating Motherhood*

"Through respectful interviews and thoughtful analysis, Chris Bobel has produced an intriguing study of mothers who engage in home schooling, alternative health care and other 'natural' maternal practices for the sake of their children and in the hope of bringing about political change. A fascinating and disturbing book."

—Sara Ruddick, author of
Maternal Thinking: Toward a Politics of Peace

"As most women search for ways to balance family life with pursuits outside the home, what happens to those who opt to devote themselves full-time and overtime to their children and families? With insight and passion, Chris Bobel shows how 'natural mothers' struggle to justify choices that may seem rebellious but are nevertheless socially constructed. By uncovering the paradoxes facing women who adopt traditional definitions of motherhood, she illuminates the tensions, contradictions, and limitations facing all contemporary women. This is a finely crafted, timely, and fascinating study."

—Kathleen Gerson, Professor and Chair,
Department of Sociology, New York University,
and author of *Hard Choices: How Women
Decide About Work, Career, and Motherhood*

The Paradox of
Natural Mothering

The
Paradox
of
Natural
Mothering

Chris Bobel

Temple University Press
PHILADELPHIA

Temple University Press, Philadelphia 19122
Copyright © 2002 by Temple University
All rights reserved
Published 2002
Printed in the United States of America

Library of Congress Cataloging-in-Publication Data

Bobel, Chris, 1963–
    The paradox of natural mothering / Christina Bobel.
    p.   cm.
    Includes bibliographical references and index.
    ISBN 1-56639-906-8 (cloth : alk. paper) — ISBN 1-56639-907-6
    (pbk. : alk. paper)
        1. Mothers—United States—Attitudes.   2. Homemakers—
    United States—Attitudes.   3. Alternative lifestyles—United States.
    4. Childbirth at home—United States.   5. Home schooling—
    United States.   I. Title.

    HQ759 .B628 2001
    306.874'3–dc21   2001027641

Contents

Acknowledgments

Ironically, as I was writing my dissertation-turned-book about families and some women's efforts to strengthen theirs, my family fell apart. It was hard writing about intact, nuclear families while mine was splitting. Nonetheless, contrasting my experience with others' gave me a perspective on how we all do the best we can with the resources we have. Mothers do not have the luxury of waiting until we feel stronger or wiser or saner before we act. We have kids, and the kids need us now.

But if we are lucky, we have people in our lives who can help us keep moving, and I have lots of those to thank here. It continually amazed me that the people surrounding me had much more confidence in my abilities than I did. In spite of my doubts, each believed I could produce not only a finished work, but a good one. For that, these individuals earned more than a mere mention on this page, but this acknowledgment is all I can offer for now.

For assuming the care of my daughter so I could write (and worry about writing) in the early stages of the project, I thank Marie Patterson. There is no better gift to a mother who works outside the home than the assurance that her child is in loving hands while she works. Virginia Woolf asserted that a woman needs a room of her own in order to write. A room is nice, but high-quality child care is truly essential.

With good humor and huge-hearted selflessness, Judy Ossers stepped in countless times, usually simply intuiting that I needed help (or rice and beans or a cheerful card). Our daughters played contentedly while our own friendship flourished. I meant it when I asked, "What will I do without you?" I still haven't figured it out. Later, the wonderful staff at Newcomb Nursery School in New Orleans played with Gracie when I couldn't. Thanks especially to Ann.

My dissertation chair, Eleanor Miller, deserves my deepest thanks for her steadfast and matter-of-fact guidance. She alone read each of my sentences in their many forms, from fragmented outlines, stream-of-consciousness e-mails, disjointed drafts, and grammatical travesties through this present incarnation. Her pride in the finished work doubles my own.

I thank the rest of my committee: Stacey Oliker, who pushed me to reckon with history and read more, more, more, and who challenged some of the most basic assumptions of my logic (I groused at the time; I thank you now); Walter Weare, whose praise for my early work meant the world; and Dale Jaffe, who nurtured me in my early days in the Urban Studies Doctoral Program, reviving my flagging confidence and providing me with outlets that moved me through the program. What I know about ethnography, I owe to you, Dale. Thanks also to Cynthia Hasbrook, who served as a helpful reader and gentle critic. Later, the expert team at Temple University Press embraced and championed the project, and I am grateful. I offer up special thanks to encouraging Michael Ames, patient Janet Francendese, efficient Janet Greenwood at Berliner, Inc., and miracle worker/copyeditor Jane Barry.

Thanks to Mary Carruth, my New Orleanian "dissertation buddy"; to colleagues from afar Mike Grover and Mark Schill, Brian Hagemann and Julie Duhigg, who kept prodding me on, playing fairy games, and solving my technical woes; to Andrea Scarpino-Prince, who actually read the whole thing (and liked it); and to the wonderful women at the University of Cincinnati Women's Center, who never doubted that I would finish and regularly picked up the slack so that I could. Thanks to Mauricio Gonzalez, my former boss, who applied just the right amount of pressure—steady but nurturing, firm but flexible. Thanks, of course, to Suzanne Cox, who also suffers from mother/scholar schizophrenia and shows me that one *can* survive and even thrive.

My family in Ohio supported me in the quiet, caring ways that families do. My little Gracie rode this creative and intellectual roller-coaster with me, although she certainly never bought the ticket. She endured my bouts of depression, desperation, and desolation, and she seldom complained. Above all, I am grateful for the perspective that having her in my life brings. My life is very different now than it was when I began this project, attesting to the predictability of change. I have Thomas to thank for appearing at the end of a long, dark tunnel, and waving his arms enthusiastically, and beckoning me out into the sunlight. It is much nicer out here. Danke.

My deepest thanks are reserved for the 32 women at the center of this study. The privilege of sitting with each as she carefully unfolded her life for my examination was a selfless gift, and I thank each of you for it. I heard your voices as I wrote and I hear them still—voices that challenge me, enlighten me, cheer me up, inspire me. You are wise women, all, and I am wiser, too, for having spent time with you.

Finally, I wish to dedicate this book to the one person who will surely never read it: my father, John Bobel (1924–1992). I know he would be proud of me, and imagining his pride and his pleasure (in another bit of irony) was often the only thing that propelled me forward. Thanks, Dad—this is for you.

The Paradox of
Natural Mothering

1 Introduction
Five Women, Five Stories

Paradoxes are the only truths.
—George Bernard Shaw

In the aisles of the local food co-op, the waiting room of the town's only homeopath, or the children's area of the public library, you might meet her. Some are inclined to label her "earth mother" or "retro hippie," but she defies categorization. One thing is certain: this woman is different. She gives birth to her babies at home; she homeschools her children; she grows much of her family's produce and sews many of their clothes. She seems at first glance an anachronism, recalling a time when women derived their identities from raising their large families and excelling at the domestic arts. But unlike the women of the past, whose domestic lives were responsive to society's dictates, today's "natural mother" resists convention. While her contemporaries take advantage of daycare, babysitters, and bottle feeding, the natural mother rejects almost everything that facilitates mother–child separation. She believes that consumerism, technology, and detachment from nature are social ills that mothers can and should oppose. This book is about these women, a population of mothers who embrace values that many would consider old-fashioned, even backward. For reasons that will become apparent as this work unfolds, I have named them "natural mothers."

1

As a feminist interested in women's experience, I wonder why such women hold this unique vision of motherhood when many American women are trying to "have it all" and break free from a gendered division of labor. Clearly, given the contemporary sociocultural context, the natural mother is radical in her approach to parenting, deviating from the majority of her cohort who are typically engaged in the struggle to combine career and family life.[1] Less obvious are the answers to questions like *why* she embraces this particular lifestyle, what motivates her to "live alternatively," what explains the origins of her commitment, and, finally, what are the implications of this style of mothering at the start of the twenty-first century.

Before I address these and related questions in depth, I want to introduce five of the 32 natural mothers I interviewed during the course of this study: Theresa Reyes, Jenny Strauss, Michelle Jones-Grant, Grace Burton, and Betsy Morehouse (all pseudonyms). Each tells a different story of coming to and sustaining a life as a natural mother. Their differences capture the range of natural mothers within my sample; their commonalities reflect the ethos that unites them. Together, their stories illustrate the themes embedded in natural mothering ideology and practice.

Michelle Jones-Grant: Reconciling Feminist Identity with Subordination to Hearth and Home

When I ring the doorbell at Michelle's house, I can see her through the window. She is barefoot, dressed in a casual jumper and holding newborn Abby in her left arm while adeptly maneuvering a vacuum over her plain wooden floors with her right. As she shuts off the vacuum, I ring the doorbell again, and Michelle heads toward the door with a toothy smile. She greets me warmly. I notice a huge bag of organic flour on the counter; it must be baking day. I comment on the quiet. She has taken her two boys, Simon, aged six, and Zeke, aged three, to her mother's nearby so we can talk uninterrupted, she explains with a wink. As we settle onto the tapestry-covered couch, Abby begins nursing, and I switch on the tape recorder. "You're gonna have loud nursing noises on your tape!" Michelle warns me good-naturedly.

"That's okay," I reply. "How did you get to this place, Michelle?"

"I have been thinking about this for the last couple of days, and I haven't come up with anything," she laughs. "You know that Talking Heads song? 'This is not my life. This is not my beautiful house. This is not my beautiful house?' I heard that song the other day, and I thought, that's me!"

As Michelle's story unfolds, I can see why her present life contradicts her original vision of the kind of life she would lead. Michelle attended a large state university, where she explored environmental politics and feminism. A "seminal" experience during that time, she tells me, was a camping trip with a boyfriend near a lake at the Canadian border. Describing the significance of her trip, Michelle seems transported:

> It changed my life. I went with a guy that I was crazy about and it was just the two of us, alone in the boundary waters for a couple weeks. And we were just completely self-sufficient. I was carrying this pack that weighed as much as I do. And we were just man and woman in the wilderness. I thought, wow, this is really cool! That could be the seminal experience. . . . There's something about just being able to take a cup, stick it in the water, and drink it that makes you feel very much like a animal. You can do anything if you can carry a canoe that weighs more than you do. It was a really powerful experience.

Around that time, Michelle began canvassing for Greenpeace and giving talks throughout the city. At one of these talks, her description of the inhumane practices of the tuna industry converted one audience member to vegetarianism. That convert was Franky, who later became Michelle's husband. While still in college, Michelle lived in a cooperative house, where she deepened her interest in vegetarianism, environmental activism, and feminism. She eventually earned a degree in women's studies. After college and marriage to Franky (who completed degrees in German, philosophy, and physics), the pair moved to a farm in Pennsylvania, where they worked as tenant farmers for three years. It was wonderful—really hard work, Michelle informs me, but "living off the land" appealed to both of them. "When it was time to make dinner, I would go into the garden and pick a tomato, pick an eggplant, and pick a green pepper and make dinner," she remembers. She made nearly all their food from scratch—bread, pasta, crackers, everything: "We bought almost no processed food." But the simple, close-to-the-earth life had its limits for the young couple. The seasonal work required odd jobs in the off–season, and their annual income of $6,000 was inadequate. After three years, Michelle and Franky returned to their home state in the upper Midwest.

Soon after returning, Michelle applied to graduate school in English, and Franky began pursuing a teaching certificate in history. But when Michelle learned that she was pregnant, she postponed her studies for a year and "just hasn't made it back yet. But if I do, I certainly won't study something as esoteric as English," she adds.

"What, then?" I ask.

"Well, probably child and family studies. Something like that. It would need to be practical."

Franky got his teaching credentials, but after a semester he discovered that teaching was too much of a psychic drain for an introvert. He decided, with Michelle's moral support, to join a friend and start a natural landscaping business. The business has been in operation for over a year and is doing quite well. Franky and his partner design, install, and maintain English-style gardens (with a minimum of pesticides) for private residences.

Although Michelle does the bookkeeping for the business at home, she identifies herself as a full-time mother. She has always worked for pay since her children were born, but never outside the home. When Simon was young, she worked as a home-based music transcriptionist (inheriting the business from a relative). "Tedious, boring work," Michelle informs me, "but it kept me right where I wanted to be, at home with my kids." She is quick to point out that she and Franky decided together that his role would be full-time breadwinner and hers full-time mother. Now that Franky is finished with school and has launched a growing business, the couple are fulfilling their "contract." At the same time, Michelle admits that her life is incredibly chaotic and stressful:

> My needs aren't getting met with my present lifestyle. My values, ah, . . . I'm living by my values, but I'm not there. I'm not in my life right now. I'm just surrounded by, just having three kids and having a newborn baby, it kind of means that you have to be gone for a while, I feel like. . . . And now, although life is really frantic and really stressful sometimes—I told Franky the other day, I feel like a blender. Somebody keeps turning me off, opening the lid, chucking something else in, and turning it back on. . . . But I still feel like I'm doing everything on my own terms, and my values are right there in front.

When I ask Michelle how she reconciles her feminist politics with her present lifestyle as a stay-at-home mother supported by a bread-winning husband, she cites her changing view of feminism:

> Well, I guess my idea of a what a feminist agenda is has really changed. I still think that things like safe, reliable, affordable birth control are really important. But I also think that being able to raise our children should be, and is for a lot of women, *the* feminist issue of the day. We want to be able to have careers, but we also want to be able to raise our own children and do things, I dunno, I guess we want it all but not, I don't know . . . I just . . . think my definition of feminism has changed just enormously. And I still feel like a feminist, although I think that, you know, to see me trooping around with my three kids, with no goal really before me beyond getting through the early years with my children, I don't look like much of a feminist.

For Michelle, raising healthy, well-adjusted children holds the best promise of making a difference in the world. Doing a good job at parenting (and for her that requires the presence of a full-time stay-at-home mother) is "the thing that's going to have the most impact on the world." When her children choose peaceful solutions to conflicts, show respect for all living creatures, and reject material measures of success, she has succeeded at "making the world a better place." But full-time, intensive, natural mothering exacts its costs. Michelle speaks of feeling isolated, feeling freakish. She wonders aloud, "If this is a movement, where are my sisters?" She felt like an "outsider" when her family chastised her for refusing to allow her first child to "cry it out." She felt alone when the hospital staff accused her of starving her baby because she insisted no bottles be given him in the nursery (to avoid "nipple confusion" and undermining her production of mother's milk).[2] And when the conservative Christian mothers in her homeschoolers group didn't understand why she doesn't attend a local church, she felt as if she "just doesn't fit anywhere." But in spite of feelings of isolation, Michelle maintains that her lifestyle, which she wholeheartedly believes she chose in the best interests of her family, is a source of power and satisfaction, endowing her with a sense of wonder at the uniqueness of the maternal–child bond:

> And you look at an entirely breastfed child who's six months old. You think, this is an amazing thing, and I did it! I am responsible for every cell of this other human being's body. Wow. Nothing compares to that for power and satisfaction. I mean, this creature, I did it. Wow! And they're perfect, you know? I created it; I made perfection. Nothing else compares.

And it is this awe that seems to move Michelle through what she herself describes as her crazy days and nights. With three children under six, she feels overwhelmed and out of touch with her own needs. But that is the *choice* she and Franky made, she reasons. Michelle's narrative reveals several key themes that run throughout the discourse of natural mothering, intersecting and informing one another: a feminist identity, the perception of choice, or personal agency, as foundational to natural mothering, and a view of natural mothering as a deliberate means to social change.

Home is where Michelle wants to be even if her role as a full-time, stay-at-home mother contradicts some of her earlier feminist notions. Because the contradiction pales in comparison with what she regards as the awesome power of motherhood, Michelle is willing to table her own needs, at least temporarily. She sees her focus on the best interests of her children as a service not only to them, but to humanity itself. Michelle's observation that "she may not look like much of a feminist" suggests that she is aware that, at least superficially, her family-centered life reaffirms patriarchal notions about the proper role for women. But, she contends, because she freely chooses to devote her energies to full-time, intensive mothering, her lifestyle is not a site of surrender, but one of resistance. For Michelle, natural mothering is social change in progress.

Theresa Reyes: Mothering the Way Nature Intended

Theresa's subdivision looks like many other suburban neighborhoods in the Midwest: ranch-style homes positioned along curvilinear roads punctuated by early-growth trees and an occasional backyard swing set. The Reyes home is modest, situated in a bedroom community populated by many families fleeing the crime, congestion, and costs of the city. I later learn that she and her husband built their home several years ago after a period of renting, and that Theresa was tenant-manager for part of that time. As I drive up, I see few people outside. Perhaps everyone is at work or school, rendering the area a virtual ghost town from nine to five. But Theresa is home, as she usually is.

I pull into the driveway wondering how this suburban residence fits in with the commitment to simplicity central to natural mothering. Once I am inside, the answer reveals itself in the relaxed feel of her home. It is clear that while space and location may be a value for the Reyes family, state-of-the-art decor and orderly living are not. The house is sparsely and modestly furnished with couches, chairs, and tables dating to the 1970s. The household furnishings are surrounded by a degree of clutter easily associated with busy people who are comfortable with piles of things. I wonder if a cluttered life contradicts the credo of simplicity. However, it appears that La Leche League's adage "people before things" is in action here, and perhaps that explains what I see.

When I pose my usual interview opener—"How did you get to this place as a mother who practices alternatives?"—Theresa replies confidently and quickly. Obviously she has considered this question before. Perhaps I am not the first to ask, or perhaps she learned long ago that those who practice an alternative lifestyle are wise to have an account prepared. Living alternatively in the context of conventionality necessitates a firm grasp on one's reasons for living outside the mainstream, and these reasons must be clear and accessible. Mothering is not something she takes lightly, after all.

After chatting briefly about her family of origin (a large Catholic family of eight) and her mother (who "tried to nurse me, but could not"), she fast-forwards to her college years. When Theresa needed a break from her graduate studies in biology at a prestigious university, she often retreated to the city's museum of art, where she wandered from painting to painting. She found herself especially drawn to the paintings of the Renaissance, in particular those depicting babies and mothers. Standing before them, she would ponder the love, serenity, and intimacy these paintings communicated. She thought, "I want that someday. I want that closeness, that bond, that unconditional love." Immersed again in her studies of human evolution, she encountered a viewpoint that resonated deeply with her experience. She distills it into a concise maxim: Whatever humans did throughout our evolutionary history and prehistory is a need programed in our genes. For Theresa, this is an indisputable truth.

Drawing on art history and biology, Theresa crafted a scientific and emotional theory in which to ground her mothering practice. Her knowledge eventually led to a new life. Disgusted with the sophistication and dishonesty of the academic world, Theresa "went exactly opposite" and married a

Portuguese man she describes as a "simple, nice country boy." Once married and nursing the first of her four children, she tells me, she realized her dream. But sustaining her positive experience of mothering required some adjustments, suggesting, ironically, that living naturally did not come naturally. Throughout her pregnancy, Theresa had planned to continue her work outside the home after the baby was born. In fact, she and her husband secured an apartment closer to her workplace so she could get to and from work more easily. But once the baby arrived, Theresa abruptly changed her mind. Mostly through nursing, she feels, she experienced a closeness to her baby she had only imagined as a graduate student. It was clear to her that she needed to be home with her baby. So the couple forfeited the security deposit on their new apartment (not a small sum for them at the time) and decided to rely exclusively on her husband's wages as a janitor and the free rent Theresa earned by serving as tenant-manager for their (new) apartment complex.

But her life as a natural mother was difficult. Her husband refused to share the household labor, believing that such tasks represented "women's work." His roles, in Theresa's words, were "companion for me, financial provider, and TV watcher." Once their fourth child was born, a desperate Theresa staged what Arlie Hochschild (1989, p. 173) has termed a "sharing showdown" and demanded that her husband either wash the nightly dishes or put the children to bed. He chose the dishes ("because that was considered the easiest of the two"), relieving some of her burden. But Theresa does not regret her life as a natural mother. Although she may not have planned to subordinate her needs to her family's, she did so because it "felt right." Above all, she believes in the "beauty of doing it the natural way" and is willing to make the sacrifices necessary to live in accordance with "nature's plan."

Theresa's is the story of a woman who struggled toward a particular vision. Natural mothering enabled her to realize her dream of feeling the close maternal–child connection she observed in Renaissance paintings, a connection she considers intrinsic, derived from nature, and therefore indisputable. Theresa expresses a twofold theme central to the ideology of natural mothering: an enduring conviction that nature is a force to be trusted and respected, coupled with steadfast deference to the "natural" bond between mother and child. In this view, nature is preeminent; in fact, nature shapes behavior. And, in this biologically determinist view, those who resist nature suffer. But in spite of these convictions, some natural mothers, like Theresa, had to make a series of adjustments so that their lives as natural mothers would "work." The fact that natural mothering doesn't "just happen" suggests that the natural life does not come "naturally." For Theresa, the necessary adjustments took the form of an apartment forgone, a job turned down, and a "sharing showdown" with her husband. And for her, it was all worth it; being a natural mother is precisely what she wanted and precisely what she got.

Michelle Jones-Grant's and Theresa Reyes's stories reveal themes that interact and produce a certain tension or ambiguity—the first of three theoretically important tensions that I will discuss. The notion that omnipotent, omniscient nature (or, more specifically, biology) shapes behavior is challenged in two distinct ways.

First, when the natural mothers speak of their *decision* to mother naturally, consistent with their identities as feminists and activists for social change through alternative living, they claim to exercise their personal agency. But certain factors mitigate against the enactment of natural mothering. To "pull it off," they make adjustments and accommodations.

But why? If this particular style of mothering were truly ordained by nature, would it not flow more freely from bodies and encounter less practical resistance? Furthermore, and more importantly, the natural mothers who characterize themselves as agents invoke a biologically determinist explanation for their particular style of mothering. The impulse to be a natural mother is intuitive, even instinctual, they assert. It is not something that can be easily explained; rather, it is the product of "just knowing" what feels right. Paradoxically, natural mothering is the choice that chooses you.

Grace Burton: Politicized Devotion to Family

An early informant told me that Grace "would be great for you to talk with" because she "is a real pioneer; she has been doing alternative stuff long before most everyone, and I am sure she has a lot of stories to tell." When I first contacted Grace to introduce myself and invite her participation, she seemed skeptical and even a bit wary. It wasn't until I mentioned my own affiliation with several groups to which Grace herself belongs that she appeared to relax. Remembering her reticence, I expected our face-to-face interview to present a challenge.

Grace meets me at the door on a cold, still winter morning. It is just before 9:00 a.m., and her small, sturdy house has the feel of a place where the morning rituals of Grace, Martin, her husband of 29 years, and their two children, Jake, age 21, and Cindy, age 16, are just getting underway. The house is cluttered, but neat. My eyes are drawn to a hammock slung between two walls. It holds a collection of twenty-something stuffed animals. A small dog—a multi-colored mutt—inhabits a large cage. I marvel at how peacefully the dog rests even as I disrupt the quiet kitchen with my entrance and the noisy setting up of tape recorder and microphones. The kitchen is plain. There are no decorations on the walls and few appliances on the counters. I do notice at least 15 bottles of vitamins, homeopathic remedies, and herbal supplements sitting on one counter.

When I ask Grace why she has chosen to live alternatively, she pauses, relaxing her broad, remarkably smooth face, and then responds confidently, "Well, I guess I am at this point in my life because I had children. I have an almost 21-year-old, and as a result of birthing that child, I began to look at the world differently." Grace tells me about attending her first La Leche League meeting. "I went for my cousin, who thought nursing might be a problem; I didn't think it would be a problem for me. I was going to nurse my baby." These were pivotal experiences, she tells me. The mothers she met at that first meeting exposed her to a style of parenting, "a nursing relationship with their children," that she could see she wanted. She became a devoted League member (reading only League-approved literature at first, she remembers, until she developed enough confidence as a mother) and later became a League leader. She laughs, "I never considered myself an organization person, and here I am, well entrenched in many organizations. . . . But I don't like organizations. My kids laugh about that."

Through her association with League, Grace began exploring practices like "family bed," homeopathy, and extended nursing.[3] She and Martin adopted the first practice: "Historically, we have slept with babies. In India, they sleep together until they leave the family." Frowning and shaking her long, straight, blondish-gray hair, she adds, "So why [family bed has] this Puritan stigma—it's really too bad." League also influenced how she birthed her second child. In 1980 her daughter was born at home, "a wonderful experience for our whole family," Grace remembers with a warm smile.

I ask what is the most radical practice she has adopted. She answers without hesitation: "Homeschooling. Why? Because it is very obvious."

> You can do long-term nursing discreetly, you can have a family bed without other people knowing, but when you say homeschooling, not only is it public, but it's public for 12 years. . . . It's there every day, and it's there for 12 years, and it's there in front of your neighbors, your parents, your siblings, the entire public school system, everybody.

Grace's story of homeschooling begins with her son's approach to kindergarten age. She had always felt that there must be some alternative to conventional schooling, but she felt compelled to send him to kindergarten at the start of the school year. But while he was off at school, she spent her free time researching homeschooling. She began with John Holt's *Teach Your Own* (1989). Her husband was incredibly supportive; in fact, it was his idea to homeschool. But it was clearly Grace's responsibility to put the idea into practice, and knowing absolutely no one who homeschooled, she lacked confidence. Martin encouraged her by saying, "How can you blow first grade? If you want to do this, do it!" So she did, and she has been homeschooling ever since. Grace remembers harsh criticism from friends, especially those who were teachers, as well as her parents and in-laws. Some chastised her for withdrawing from an imperfect school system, asking, "Wouldn't it be better to work in the system and improve education for all kids?" To that, Grace responds:

> I wouldn't be real good at trying to work with the system to change the system. I'm not a very assertive person. The other thing was that I had my experience through home birth. I just

> didn't have the time to wait for the system to figure out how to do it right for my child. You know, people said, "Well, why don't you just work within the system?" I didn't have time to do that. . . . It's my child we're working with here!

Grace's sense of urgency and the premium she places on the immediate well-being of her family come through loud and clear during our conversation. She is passionate, growing agitated when the topic is especially meaningful to her. As we talk, I watch her prepare a loaf of raisin bread to bring to a potluck that evening. She kneads the dough, pounding and tugging at it as she explains her frustration with impersonal social services (she recently took her elderly aunt to apply for state assistance), her disillusionment with a women's movement she thinks forces mothers to work outside the home, and her impatience with social labels of all kinds. As she folds a cup of raisins into the kneaded dough, she reveals her exasperation with the ways in which the Reagan-Bush years impoverished American families, especially middle-class ones. Grace believes that special tax credits for households where mothers stay home with the children would help families channel their energies back to home and hearth. Part of the problem, she suggests, is that we, as a culture, evaluate our worth against a materialist standard:

> Parked in front of the public elementary school down the street, I see these smart little energy-efficient economy cars with baby car seats strapped in the back, and I think those mothers probably feel they are doing everything right—conserving energy, serving schoolchildren, bringing money into their families. But their babies are not with their mothers, and that's not okay.

Grace asserts that parents and children are forced apart to satisfy the parents' needs for material gain. She and Martin have resisted the compulsion to live beyond their means. For instance, when the young couple house-hunted many years ago, the realtors continually pressured them to purchase the kind of house whose mortgage would require two incomes. But Grace knew she didn't want to spend that much money on a home. She wanted her flexibility: "I knew people who got caught in those kinds of traps, where they had this big, expensive home. We tell people how much money you need for a family of four to survive, and then that's how much you need. And if you don't have that much money, you can't."

Yet Grace seems sympathetic to families who find themselves trapped in a unforgiving and relentless cycle of work-consume-work. From Grace's perspective, parents are too overworked and exhausted to prepare a meal from scratch or spend quality *and* quantity time with their children, so they order takeout and hire babysitters—spending money that has to be replenished through more of the work that exhausted them in the first place.

At this point, Grace falls silent as she expertly separates the dough into three equal parts, rolls them into three long snakes, and braids them into an elegant twisted loaf. A dusting of flour is swiped across her blouse, and there is a bit on her cheek. I try to imagine her as a college student and as the woman who worked in corporate banking and accounting for eight years before she had children. "You know mothers and babies need to be together," she continues, "and I think mothers can heal themselves by being with their babies. When you hold your crying baby, the crying baby inside yourself can feel held."

She has heard the critics of her attached style of parenting, who worry that such a child-centered family practice makes women invisible because they are continually subordinating their needs to her children's. "Ideally, if we had a community of women who shared mothering and supported one another, mothering wouldn't seem such a drain, such a burden," Grace offers in response. But it's a matter of perspective. "Sure, mothers need to meet their needs, but they don't need to be separated from their babies to meet those needs." Our society expects parents and children to be separate at public functions, but Grace and Martin accommodated conflicting parent and child needs differently: "We took our children everywhere we went, and if the children were not welcome, we didn't go." Her priority, she reiterates, is and always will be the well-being of her family.

Just then her son, Jake, appears, and Grace introduces us. He is tall and lanky, wearing wire-rim glasses and sporting freshly combed shoulder-length hair. Dressed in jeans and a flannel shirt, Jake heads for the refrigerator as Grace points out the stack of sandwiches on the top shelf and the bag of apples in the crisper. She turns to me, "He is going on a retreat overnight." Turning back to Jake, she adds with a smile, "And there's oatmeal cookies on the counter."

"Okay. Thanks," replies Jake. I wonder to myself if she typically prepares his sack lunches; he seems accustomed to her care.

We continue talking about what she believes new mothers need (food and support, not fancy things for the baby or high-tech medical care) and how people regard her as a deviant for choosing to treat her family's health-care problems with alternative therapies, like herbs and homeopathy. "We are considered quacks," she confides, "and I realize that virtually every choice I make is political. I consider myself a real radical, a radical feminist." Just then, the doorbell rings. It is Jake's friend (and his ride to the retreat). Grace abruptly excuses herself and jumps up to say goodbye to her son. I hear whispers exchanged between them, then an audible, "Goodbye. Have a good time."

When she returns and settles back into her chair, we talk about my impressions of alternative families as *led* by mothers. It seems it is the mothers and not the fathers who typically initiate homeschooling, I suggest. Yes, Grace agrees. Mothers tend to be at the forefront of change in the context of the family. By virtue of being home more than fathers and unshackled from the oppressive workplace, mothers are freer to open themselves to alternatives.

As we shift to the potential of natural mothers to reshape families and shuffle cultural priorities, Grace speaks of the small-scale, person-by-person mode of change in which she puts her own faith. Eight years ago, a reporter from a local paper—pregnant at the time—interviewed Grace regarding some pending homeschooling legislation. Grace, with her characteristic passion, imparted her philosophy of education (you can't make a person learn) and the benefits of homeschooling (it allows children to learn at their own pace). Later, she learned that the reporter quit her job to stay at home with her new baby, joined La Leche League, and became a leader. Now she is considering homeschooling— "All as a result of that interview."

"How did that make you feel?" I query.

"Kind of scared," Grace replies. "But neat also, because I just talked with her, the same as I am talking with you, and obviously it was something she must have wanted to do, and I just supported her."

And supporting others in "doing what they want to do" has been Grace's goal during her mothering career. But before she could extend her reach to others, she first had to find her own "truths"—truths she ultimately located in nature. Grace forged ahead as a rare homeschooling parent in the 1970s. As her children grew, so did her conviction that children and mothers should remain together, consistent with nature's plan. She faults a contemporary culture tragically seduced by consumption for setting in motion the relentless spend-work-spend cycle that alienates mothers from children. In Grace's view, she and her family stand proudly as an exception to this rule. Grace's critique of consumer society (reminiscent of similar critiques expressed by other natural mothers) represents another important theme. Throughout our interviews, mother after mother implicated the social fixation on "biggering and bettering" (as one mother put it) as the root of societal dysfunction and individual unhappiness. The natural mothers, on the whole, believe that their disapproval of hyper-materialism sets them apart from mainstream culture—a separation of which they are proud.

Jenny Strauss: The Sequenced Life of a Stay-At-Home Mother

Leaning over the kitchen counter in her bright and cluttered kitchen, Jenny, clad in a nylon jogging suit, is putting the finishing touches on a key lime pie. She chuckles to herself:

> I am taking this to a birthday party tonight. I just got off the phone with the guest of honor because I don't know her very well, but I had a hunch that her crowd would be a very organic, vegetarian one, you know? And I didn't know if she would want to have a birthday cake, or if anyone would bring one. She was so happy I asked and is really looking forward to my bringing this pie. You know, I go to these functions all the time, and there's never any dessert! I went to a summer picnic not long ago, a home birth picnic—all these kids there—and not a single dessert. Where are the brownies? Where are the chocolate chip cookies? It's interesting the way my life has evolved.

Jenny's evolution as a natural mother has been slow and steady. Unlike others I spoke with, she had not planned on having children, much less on raising them alternatively. When Jenny and Dave began their courtship as mere 14-year-olds, they resolved that they would never have children. Together, they imagined a life defined by satisfying careers—physical therapy for her, engineering for him—free from the constraints on spontaneity and mobility that invariably come with parenting. "For a long time in my life I was sure I was never going to have any kids. I was dead certain of that for probably 10 years out of my life," Jenny recalls, describing the period from her high school courtship with Dave until her mid-twenties. But if you look at Jenny and Dave's life today, it is clear that the child-free plans of their youth gave way to a different vision, one not only populated with three active boys, ages 14, 11, and 6, but _defined by_ their commitment to their children. Dave is an engineer who designs air-conditioning systems; Jenny, a proud self-defined stay-at-home mother who runs two businesses out of her home while her children are at school. Obviously, something, or perhaps someone, changed their minds about children. Jenny is not sure what. She only knows that slowly she and Dave decided that they would like to have children after all.

When they began their family, Jenny recalls "starting from scratch," since having children was not anything she had planned on doing. Looking for guidance, Jenny turned to books, where, among other things, she first encountered the notion of family bed—"a totally new concept." Later, Jenny found her way to a meeting of La Leche League so that she could meet other women with babies, since she didn't know a single nursing mother. Pregnant with her first child, Jenny knew she wanted to breastfeed. Her family had a significant history of allergies, and she had read that breastfeeding would reduce the child's chances of having them.

Encountering a three- or four-year-old who climbed into his mother's lap to nurse, she was totally astounded. "Holy cow!" she thought. "This is really weird; this is *really* weird."

But it wasn't long before Jenny herself was exposing League initiates to the practice of extended nursing and a plethora of parenting alternatives. In partnership with another natural mother, Jenny works as a labor assistant to women who choose natural birth, in both home and hospital settings. She also teaches Bradley childbirth education classes (many of her labor-assistance clients come from her pool of childbirth students).[4] Through her birth practice, both as labor assistant and as educator (roles that regularly overlap), she provides information to families interested in natural health care, breastfeeding, family bed, whole foods, and stay-at-home motherhood. Her second business is a partnership with her husband. Together, they market and sell a form of edible algae touted as an all-natural, completely safe miracle food. "Super Blue-Green Algae," she passionately explains, boosts energy levels, heals topical wounds, and generally improves one's quality of life. This product is growing in popularity within the alternative health and whole foods communities, Jenny points out, and at the close of our interview she gives me the soft sell. Both businesses keep her quite busy. In a remarkable turnabout, the woman who imagined a life without children is now wholly committed to natural birthing and alternative health care within her own family and the alternative community beyond.

Jenny herself characterizes her evolution as a "multiple child process." Fourteen years ago her first child had a conventional hospital birth (she believed home birth was unsafe). Once home, the baby slept in a crib all but the first two weeks of his life. Her second, also born in a hospital, spent his first two months in the family bed, advanced to a bedside bassinet, and ultimately moved to a crib. But her third and final child was born at home with no intervention and slept alongside Jenny in the family bed for the first nine months. Now a proponent of home birth and family bed, Jenny muses, "Once you believe it, it's the obvious choice, and once you believe it, it's very hard to go back to where you were before and think, 'Why did I think that was safe?'"

Similarly, when Jenny first encountered homeopathy, her reaction was, "Weird, very weird." Seeing "those little white bottles" on a friend's bathroom counter for years, she remained ignorant and skeptical. But when a local naturo-pathic physician offered a class on homeopathic remedies in pregnancy, Jenny, as a childbirth educator/assistant, felt a professional obligation to attend. Soon thereafter, she began dispensing homeopathic remedies to her children and even-tually to her "suspicious" husband, who was converted when he was "miraculously cured" of a miserable sore throat by the contents of one of Jenny's little white bottles. Now he, too, embraces alternative medicine.

What Jenny's conversion to natural mothering lacked in speed, it has made up for in conviction. And this conviction extends beyond the realm of individual preference. She boldly voices her vehement opposition to mothers' working outside the home. In her view, daycare inevitably sacrifices children's needs to accommodate mothers'. Earlier in Jenny's parenting career, she placed her own children in daycare, and at the time, she says, she "had the luxury of thinking, 'This is actually good.'" But she made sacrifices in her job to minimize the sacrifices of her family. Jenny worked part-time as a physical therapist and sat at her desk eating a peanut butter sandwich while her co-workers went off to lunch each day. As she relates this story, her resent-ment toward her peers who claimed that they *had* to work is evident. She dismisses that claim as self-delusion, one she shed as her family grew. Since she began working as a private labor assistant, she has sometimes found it necessary to place her youngest son in daycare when she is called to attend a client's birth. But, she is quick to add, "I could no longer fool myself . . . that this was actually quality time for him." As for mothers of young children in daycare who believe that it is good for children to interact and develop relationships with caregivers other than their mothers, Jenny fumes, "That is total bullshit. We kid ourselves."

At this point, Jenny excuses herself for a moment, walks into the kitchen, and returns carrying a bag of precut, prewashed carrots. Setting them before us, she continues: "I think the present generation of kids raised in daycares will haunt us. I think it is an illusion that this generation of kids can somehow adapt to what we're asking them to adapt to and come out okay at the end."

She faults a culture that teaches today's mothers that it "really is okay to go out and meet your needs." At the same time, she recognizes that a lot of mothers internalize guilt when they do pursue careers and make daycare arrangements for their children. That guilt, Jenny believes, does not come from "outside," as she puts it, but from "inside." It reflects a deep-seated discomfort with combining career and family. Mothers intuitively know that their children need them at home providing full-time care. Their statements about needing a second paycheck or the benefits of daycare centers as outlets for children and forums for positive peer socialization are mere rationalizations. In Jenny's view, anything short of full-time motherhood is a disservice to children and a product of self-delusion.

While Jenny pauses, reaching for another carrot and taking a last sip of tea, I scan the living room where we sit.

Jenny reclines on a well-worn couch in a neutral shade, and I find myself in a overstuffed upholstered chair. A hodge-podge assortment of chairs are arranged in no particular order, except for two straight-backed chairs positioned directly in front of the television. Jenny notices the direction of my gaze and explains, "David and I love *ER* and never miss it on Thursday nights. It's our standing date."

Jenny has achieved a certain mother–child togetherness while maintaining a professional life through a mothering strategy called "sequencing." Coined by Arlene Rossen Cardozo in 1985, the term "sequencing" refers to a lifestyle approach in which women recognize that they can "have it all, but not all at once," in Jenny's paraphrase. Cardozo describes a woman's life as entailing a series of events that track the development of her children. Mothers who sequence typically interrupt their careers so that they can be home full-time with their children, rejecting the "Super-mom" myth that, according to Cardozo, the women's move-ment constructed and promoted as the solution to gender inequity. Jenny summarizes the book's message this way:

> It talks about having it all but not all at once. I mean, parent-ing children is really not that big of a part in our lives, but when they're little it seems like forever. I can look at my 14-year-old and think, man, if I had only one child, he would be at the point now where I could have this incredible profes-sional career. . . . So, that was the neat thing about the *Sequenc-ing* book, because it talked about how you really can have it all, you just can't have it all at once. Because it isn't humanly possible to do it all at once and do any of it very well.

But Jenny has not sequenced. Her children are now away at school full-time, but the structure of her life remains largely unchanged. Why not return to her work in physical therapy? I ask. She answers simply: Because she does not want to: "It's interesting, because I'm home now more for me than my kids. I mean, I really could be out there doing something five or six hours a day. It's like, I have no desire to do that. I really do not, money or not. I have really absolutely no desire as a person to do that."

To my probe, "Why not?" Jenny replies:

> My life is so cluttered and full when the kids are around that it's like this blissful sanctuary to have them trot off to school. Last week the school had their fundraising auction, and I sat around making key lime tarts for the auction. I thought, boy, isn't this just the classic stereotype of the stay-at-home mom! Here I am, baking for the bake sale, and it was like, it was heavenly, because I hardly ever have time in my days to do that. . . . But there was something real comforting about doing that bake sale baking. It just really resonated with something inside, like, Oh, I remember my mom doing this when I was a kid. . . . It just feels really good to be homemaking. A lot of what I do at home isn't homemaking, it's business stuff or volunteer stuff, or cleaning stuff, which never feels very homemaking. It's not nurturing; it's just grunge. Somebody's got to wash the walls, vacuum the floors.

And it appears that usually that someone is Jenny. But she doesn't sound resentful that her days are filled with "grunge" interrupted by the occasional "heavenly" activity. Because she places such a premium on stay-at-home motherhood, she is willing to do what it takes to provide for her family in the way she deems best. "Well, it's clear to me as a society we don't value children. I mean, we pay a lot of lip-service, but we don't. We truly do not value children. And it's scary to me, watching what's happening to the kids that are growing up right now," she states passionately.

It is striking to hear such strong sentiments from the mouth of a woman who never imagined children in her life, a woman who set herself on a career path that did not involve children at all. Today, Jenny's life is consumed with children, both in her own mothering practice and in her work to support mothering and stay-at-home mothers. This personal transformation is not an uncommon experience for natural mothers. Jenny's tale, in fact, represents another key theme central to an understanding of natural mothering—the theme of conversion, expressed through something I loosely term "shock-shift stories." Because Jenny came to feel so strongly about a mother's responsibility to her children, rooted in the unique bond between mother and child, she was willing to restructure her life to minimize separation from her three boys. This effort entailed founding two home-based businesses, both of which target natural mothers like herself. Jenny, as we have seen, vehemently criticizes mothers who place their own needs before their children's and prescribes a way for them to avoid this mistake. Sequencing requires carving a woman's life into stages: the career/premothering stage, the mothering stage, and the postmothering/career-revisited stage. For mothers like Jenny who subordinate their needs, at least temporarily, to their families', sequencing is a viable strategy.

The themes embedded in Jenny's story and Grace Burton's reveal a second theoretical tension. The natural mothers believe that they have wrested control of their personal lives away from institutions and experts and others who claim to "know best" and returned it to the site of the individual family. I argue, however, that this hard-won control does not rest with the individual; rather, it is surrendered to nature. The natural mothers exalt nature as a force to be trusted and respected, and this realization sometimes shocks them. Subsequently, they shift their perspective, relinquishing control to nature, restructuring their lives, and sometimes "sequencing" their careers. Few sacrifices seem too large.

While the women claim that their lives as natural mothers resist a set of social beliefs derived from mainstream culture, they uncritically accept a different but nonetheless powerful belief in naturalism. This culture/nature dualism merely passes control from one socially constructed authority to another, revealing another paradox: By deferring to nature as the supreme authority, the natural mothers contradict their claim that the *individual* must determine the substance of family life. Natural mothering, then, simultaneously resists and accepts a force larger than the mother herself.

Betsy Morehouse: The Struggle for Alternative Identity

"I am embarrassed to tell you where I work," Betsy tells me. "It's a humiliating job. It's minimum-wage, and I hate it." It hasn't always been like this for Betsy. Thirty-two and the mother of Liam, four and a half, she admits that her daily existence as a single mother trying to "nurture and at the same time scratch out a living" is a struggle. She is soft-spoken, but her frustration with poverty and the lack of practical and emotional support echoes through her quiet demeanor. Her thin frame is covered by simple, well-worn clothes that she informs me came from thrift stores. "I like old things," she explains. She wears one black sock and one blue, retro horn-rimmed glasses, and no makeup. Her long, straight brown hair is tied back in a ponytail. She looks tired and worried; I want to know why.

One of six children (a sister also practices natural mothering), Betsy has always been working-class. When she was 26 and living in Minneapolis, she met Patrick and became pregnant with Liam. This was an unplanned but not unwelcome pregnancy. Patrick's alcoholism led Betsy to Al-Anon, which helped her reevaluate their relationship. She eventually left

Patrick, deeming him extremely unhealthy for both herself and Liam. Currently, she is attempting to eliminate unsupervised visitation for Patrick because she fears that Liam feels responsible for his father.

After splitting up with Patrick, Betsy relocated to a mid-sized city where one of her sisters was living. Soon after the move, Betsy and Liam, then two and a half, moved into a downtown co-op. She says, "It was really hard for me, but it was also really very fun and I still miss it so much. I know that that is how I want to live." The house was not structurally kid-friendly, and a number of the residents did not seem to like having a child around. Still, living simply in the context of a stable intentional community appealed to Betsy, and she aspires to find another co-op soon. "Community is what I want," she says. When Betsy and Liam lived in the co-op, they had a room "a bit more than half the size of this living room," she tells me, gesturing to what I consider a small room in a tiny one-bedroom apartment. As Betsy talks, I scrutinize the apartment for signs of her life. I notice the mountain bike leaning against the wall (75 dollars at a yard sale, she tells me, and their only mode of transportation). I notice the peeling paint, the crumbling plaster, and the broken flooring. She catalogs her possessions for me: "That chair I got off the street . . . and that futon. That dresser we got in the co-op. That table my dad made. Mostly," she summarizes, "we get our stuff off the street, from people's curbs."

As I scan the room, the upstairs tenant begins drumming so loudly that the noise nearly drowns out Betsy's words. She smiles feebly and continues, "But I wouldn't have all this stuff if I weren't lonely. The stuff just fills up the loneliness." It doesn't look like much stuff to me, I say to myself, reevaluating my own preoccupation with material comforts.

And the drumming continues, an intrusion I suspect Betsy has learned to live with.

Betsy went on public assistance before Liam was born and continued receiving Aid to Families with Dependent Children (AFDC) until recently. Her eyes darting, she says she felt fine about receiving public aid so she could be a full-time mother. "Being a mom to Liam gave me a lot of self-esteem, but then when he turned two and a half, the state made me go to work, and so I had to put him in daycare." That arrangement—Betsy at work and Liam in daycare—persists today. Currently, they receive only food stamps, Medical Assistance, and Section 8 housing support, which makes it possible for Betsy to afford their apartment. She has worked on and off as a waitress, a job she likes and "can make a lot of cash" doing, but currently she works as a clerk at a brewing supply store:

> I work all day at this job where they expect you to be there all the time, that's how it is with these minimum-wage jobs, and then when I get off, I need some time to myself, but then I have to go pick up Liam and he is really needy, understand-ably, and we get home and it's five-thirty or six, and then we're starving and the house is cold, so we don't really eat . . . sometimes I just feel so overwhelmed. I haven't gotten my food stamps for about three months because it's humiliating.

We talk about what it means to practice alternative parenting and be poor and single. Betsy nursed Liam until he was three and a half, and a lot of that time, she tells me, she hated nursing: "I would lay there nursing him to sleep, and I'd be gritting my teeth, and I'd be thinking, 'I hate this! I hate this! I hate this!'" It would have been easier if someone had been there to support her, to hold her, to give her back rubs, she explains. But reasoning, "No one gives a fuck about me, so fuck them; he's not going to nurse until he's five," she weaned Liam—still long after most American mothers have ceased breastfeeding.

She and Liam are vegetarians and try to eat as healthfully as her budget permits. Betsy buys as much organic produce as she can from the local food co-op. As a volunteer at the co-op, she has access to the free food box, which helps a lot, but it's hard for her to eat well, especially when she often feels alone in her commitment to a whole foods diet. For instance, when she and Liam lived in the YWCA for a time, a group of the other mothers would fry chicken every night while Betsy prepared a meal of brown rice and tahini sauce or sweet potatoes and fried onions and garlic. As Liam gravitated toward the chicken dinners, the women would tease Betsy: "He hates your food. Ha ha. He wants our food!"

Recently, Liam nearly lost his finger when a window in their apartment slammed shut on his hand. Betsy debated whether to give him the antibiotics the emergency room physician prescribed. She feared that if she did not administer the drug and Liam's finger became infected, she would be accused of being "a stupid, minimum-wage moron." She refused the antibiotics, largely because her boyfriend supported her decision: "If he hadn't been there, I bet I would have given them to him." But Betsy's uncertainty about food and health care is clearly the result of her limited resources. She displays no doubt about what is best for children, only what is possible in her situation. Her ideas about a child's need to be kept close and placed at the center of a family's attention were drawn from a book known to nearly all the natural mothers I interviewed. *The Continuum Concept,* based on Jean Liedloff's two-year immersion in a South American jungle with people she labels "Stone Age Indians," prescribes an alternative model of parenting that relies on continuous mother–baby contact, including extended breastfeeding, "wearing your baby" (in a device like a shoulder sling or front pack), and sharing sleep in a family bed. "I remember I cried through [the book] when I realized what I didn't get," Betsy recalls painfully. But her notions about mothering do not derive solely from books; in fact, she suggests that they transcend the intellectual. Books like Liedloff's, in combination with Betsy's contact with La Leche League, gave rise to a cluster of ideas that "just made sense," she says. "I was surrounded by people who were doing things differently. I just never thought about it. I just sort of knew."

Betsy Morehouse's story—that of a single mother living below the poverty line—resounds with struggle. She imagines a better life supported by an intentional community someday. For now, she labors in what she considers a "humiliating job" and worries each time she makes a choice about health care that might be questioned by some authority with a different attitude toward childrearing. Betsy, like so many of the mothers discussed earlier, speaks of "just knowing" that a particular mothering practice "felt right." But while the natural mothers rely on their "intuition" as a practical guide, they are fully aware that their approach to mothering is at odds with mainstream notions about the proper way to raise a family. And this tension between what is felt and what is expected produces risk.

This theme of risk recurs throughout the natural mothers' discourse, although the specifics differ from mother to mother. While Betsy worries that a physician will criticize her for rejecting conventional medical treatment, Michelle Jones-Grant evaluates the toll her intensive natural mothering takes on her psyche. Michelle often feels out of control (like a blender whirling at top speed), but reasons that the risks of this crazy, spinning life are worth the gains to her children, and ultimately the planet.

privilege

Betsy's tale of struggle raises an intriguing question: Is natural mothering dependent on privilege? Betsy's constraints—poverty, a dearth of social support, fatigue, and self-doubt—make it difficult for her to enact the choices she "feels" are best for her and Liam. And sometimes she is acutely aware of how separate she is from the natural mothering peers she relates to ideologically if not materially. Betsy's narrative is important because the absences in her tale—an adequate income, social capital, and familial support, especially that of a partner—illuminate the givens in the tales of most natural mothers. Michelle, Theresa, Jenny, and Grace represent the majority of natural mothers, who enjoy a certain set of privileges based on class, race, and marital status, and this position of privilege is yet another theme central to natural mothering.

Betsy's narrative and its implicit themes force us to reckon with a third and final tension: the contradictory nature of natural mothering as a social movement. The mothers themselves are confident that their lives are advancing social change, albeit on a micro-level. Their very existence as mothers who place a premium on simplicity and family togetherness challenges the status quo, they contend. Grace Burton, for instance, muses: "I've decided that absolutely everything I do is political." Regarding diet, health care, and schooling for her two children, Grace has always made choices that resonate with her values, and a majority of natural mothers similarly conceive of their style of mothering as a political enterprise. Their approach is reminiscent of the nineteenth-century reformers who also championed maternity and domesticity—and in this case too the potential for social change is limited. Natural mothering may resist certain capitalist and technological prescriptions for family life, but it does not resist essentialized, even romanticized, conceptions of women that manifest themselves in a rigid sexual division of labor.

The route to natural mothering is different for each woman. Yet certain themes serve as common markers along the varied paths. These themes intersect to produce three interrelated tensions. Although the natural mothers themselves do not necessarily experience these tensions or contradictions as such, they are essential to a full and complex understanding of natural mothering.

Chapter 2 presents a brief history of American female moral reform as a background for understanding natural mothering. Celebration of maternity as an essentialized practice and a route to social change is consistent with, and arguably derived from, the rich and controversial history of maternalist reform movements in America.

Chapter 3 breaks down natural mothering into its practical and ideological components: Voluntary Simplicity, Attachment Parenting, and Cultural Feminism. In Chapters 4, 5, and 6, I examine what natural mothering means to the mothers themselves—how they understand what they do and why they do it—drawing heavily on the informants' own words. Here I explore the ideology that guides natural mothering practice and especially certain key thematic tensions. The first, detailed in Chapter 4, centers on socially constructed choice versus biological destiny. Chapter 5 describes the tension inherent in a position that simultaneously tries to wrest control of mothering from "mainstream" culture and surrender it to nature. The third tension, discussed in Chapter 6, derives from the movement's commitment to effect social change at the same time that it accommodates patriarchal constructions of womanhood and motherhood and depends largely on privilege for its enactment. Throughout the explorations of these related tensions, we will continually uncover the internally contradictory discourse of natural mothering as simultaneously regressive and progressive.

BELOW is what The
5 women; 5 stories — 5 MOTHERS have
To sAy:

10. subordinate needs, "felt Right"

11. "natural mothering doesn't "just happen" suggests that the natural life does not come "naturally."

11. Themes That present certain tensions.

12. "If This particular style of mothering were truely ordained by NATURE, would it not Flow more freely from Bodies and encounter less practical resistance?"
→ Gus would say That even The "UN-NATural" is natural.

13. Birthing a child / look at the world differently.

15. disillusionment w/ a women's movement that forces women To work outside the home.

15. parents are and children are forced apart to satisfy The parent's need for material gain.

16. Unrelentless cycle of work-consume-work.

16. critics of attachment parenting: "makes women invisible" (But isn't This Because we don't have a community of like-minded women to give support?)

17. every choice is political.

18. mothers tend to Be at the forefront of change in the family.

20. defined By Their commitment to their children.

22. resentment toward peers who say The have to work — dismisses That claim as self-delusion.

23. present generation of children raised in dAycares will come to haunt us.

2 Female Moral Reform and the Maternal Politics of Accommodation

The thread of female moral reform runs through American history from the late eighteenth century up to the present. It has manifested itself in a variety of forms, including the antiabortion movement (see Ginsberg, 1989) and, I argue, natural mothering.[1]

The story of female moral reform begins with a wave of Protestant religious revivals known as the Second Great Awakening (1797–1840). The revivals provided women with a female network of peers and armed them with "an ability to understand the world in new terms, from a standpoint that was centered in women's experience and critical of society as it was" (Epstein, 1981, p. 6; cf. Cott, 1977). Because the revivalists' social critique stopped short of confronting the masculinist bias of Christianity, women involved in the revivals both rebelled and submitted. At the center of their Christianity, however, was "accommodation to the inevitable—male dominance" (Epstein, 1981, p. 87).

The religiously defined world view women adopted during the period of the revivals championed a domesticity that they saw threatened by a new social order shaped by an evolving cash-based economy. The Industrial Revolution transformed the organization of work and, in turn, the American family. A system of more fluid, task-based roles gave way to a rigidly defined division of labor. Women and men, particularly within the middle class, legitimated these changes by linking them to distinct gender roles (Cott, 1977) rooted in a belief that women and men are naturally different.

Some historians argue that women's domestic attachments presented a paradox (see Cott, 1977; Epstein, 1981; Ryan, 1981). Domesticity brought material comfort and refuge from the difficult and perplexing economic world, and it permitted women to exert their moral influence. Simultaneously, however, it committed women to a limited range of roles. In spite of romantic and sentimental rhetoric celebrating the domestic life, home life was difficult, lonely, and filled with drudgery. Faced with limited possibilities, "women faced an overwhelming irony: they were to choose their bondage" (Cott, 1977, p. 78). The gendered division of labor not only redefined roles for women and men but exaggerated gender differences. Still, the same bonds that tied women to what became known as "women's sphere" also tied women to one another (Cott, 1977). Domesticity in this era was a mixed blessing.

As the nineteenth century progressed and the sexual division of labor became more entrenched, an emphasis on motherhood emerged as the locus of women's domesticity. This maternal focus marked a real departure from Puritanical constructions of the family, in which fathers handled the religious, moral, and intellectual development of children and motherhood was but one of many womanly tasks.[2] In contrast, the nineteenth century view saw motherhood as women's most important, almost sacred, responsibility. Children, once viewed as a source of labor, were now "priceless," seen as a testimony to moral worth (Zelitzer, 1985).

The emphasis on motherhood as the source of women's identity and fulfillment had a material basis. Stripped of the duties women once performed as an integral part of the household economy (such as the production of goods and services within the home-based agrarian economy), middle-class women found that the only creative and challenging work left to them was motherhood (Gordon, 1977, as cited in Ginsberg, 1989). Nancy Cott (1977), however, traces the new focus on motherhood as women's primary vocation to the rhetoric of early nineteenth-century New England ministers who stressed the importance of mothers to the well-being of the church and the solidity of the faith. Motherhood was further sanctified in an emerging ideology of separate spheres known retrospectively as the "cult of true womanhood" (Welter, 1976). By prescribing a set of four cardinal virtues thought to be incompatible with the demands of the "outside world"—piety, purity, submissiveness, and domesticity—the ideology secured men's exclusive place in the formal labor market (Welter, 1976).

As I suggest above and many contemporary critics have shown (see, for instance, hooks [1984]), the "cult" was a particularly middle-class construction. In fact, Joseph Gusfield (1986) argues that the middle class embraced certain values in order to establish itself as respectable and distinct from newer immigrants, whereas Cott believes that the ideal of true womanhood "implied a repudiation of aristocratic models . . . [thus assigning] the domestic vocation as a leveling vocation for *all* women (1977, p. 93, emphasis mine). Clearly the cult of true womanhood merits discussion for its reflection of cultural notions about women's roles, even if only middle-class women were equipped to meet its dictates.[3]

In spite of some early feminist detractors, most (white, middle- and upper-class) women appeared content with their circumscribed roles (Welter, 1976).[4] Moreover, it would be inaccurate, Barbara Epstein cautions (1981), to assume that nineteenth-century women were victims of false consciousness when they embraced the limitations of "women's sphere." Women of earlier generations, as well as poor women and others deprived of male support, may well have envied the middle- and upper-class "hostage of the home." And, Epstein proposes, "at least in an immediate sense it was in women's best interest to play as large a part as possible in defining the domestic role in establishing the content and ideology of domesticity" (p. 84). Women could even lay claim to a circumscribed arena of authority through being seen as men's moral and religious superiors. But the ideology of separate spheres and the cult of true womanhood were hardly benign. Cott argues that these interlocking ideologies not only failed to confront the organization of work and pursuit of wealth, but also "accommodated and promised to temper them" (1977, p. 69; see also Gusfield, 1986).

As forces of industrialization and commercialization continued to dismantle the home-based agrarian economy, women's proper domain was seen as extending beyond the home into the community, and their sphere was more loosely defined as the arena of morality. Movements for social reform, utopianism, industrialization, and westward expansion compelled women to participate in more worldly affairs by appealing to their status as "social purists." After all, if woman was the "chosen vessel" filled with superior morality and unparalleled virtue, was it not her mission to rid the world of its vices? Perhaps the best example of this principle in action was the work of the Female Moral Reform Society (FMRS). Founded in the 1830s and prominent for a full decade, the FMRS attacked sexual misconduct and pushed for more responsible personal ethics. Many of its core organizers were veterans of the second wave of the evangelical revivals, although the diverse membership included married and unmarried women from all social and economic classes.[5]

As the nineteenth century progressed, women's love of associations as vehicles of social change grew and encompassed an ever-broadening range of issues. In Mary Ryan's words, "the sphere was not a home" any longer, and now women had forced their way into various "labors of love"— professional tasks, social welfare, and ministering to the problems generated by industrial society (1981, p. 186). Women "had taken up an extra-domestic role in social reproduction, acting to help maintain, socialize, and replenish the work force for industrial society" (p. 212). Ironically, as women enacted their moral "superiority" in the public domain, they simultaneously legitimated the ideology that confined women to domestic (albeit expanded) roles (Thurer, 1994).

There were still limits to this newly extended sphere. Women attempted to extend their influence beyond church and charity into organized politics, "rough and rugged labor, the publicity of the platform and pulpit, the conflict of hustings, the senate-house, and the forum" (Ryan, 1981, p. 188). Even the saloon was not off-limits. Women regarded drunkenness, particularly male drunkenness, as the root of many social evils and a real threat to the sanctity of home and hearth. At the same time, temperance was a "symbolic crusade" whereby new immigrant groups were differentiated from one another and, most importantly, from the first wave of American immigrants (see Gusfield 1986). The pursuit of temperance, in this view, was actually a pursuit of a distinct and privileged social status. To this end, women (largely descendents of first-wave immigrants, it must be noted) invoked the belief in their moral and religious superiority and nurturant nature in founding the Woman's Christian Temperance Union (WCTU) in 1874. The WCTU rode the wave of enthusiasm for its single issue into a widened political activism spanning range of issues, including labor and social welfare (Epstein, 1981, especially pp. 114–46). Although many temperance reforms were temporary, the organizational skills and sisterhood generated by these efforts extended women's sphere beyond the confines of the home and demonstrated that female moral reformers could respond to the economic and political realities of their time.

In the 1870s, women reformers turned their attention to controlling reproduction, creating the "voluntary motherhood movement." Reformers promoted various natural birth control measures but opposed abortion, fearing that it would promote male promiscuity by protecting men from the consequences of their sexual activity (Gordon, 1977, as cited in Ginsberg, 1989, p. 232). Other efforts were directed toward gaining admission to the nation's colleges for women and creating women-only institutions. Reformers argued that women would be better mothers and wives if educated (Rossiter, 1982, p. 1). New graduates were infused into the burgeoning suffrage movement. As women rallied for the vote, they employed familiar rhetorical themes, asserting that women's suffrage would lead to a moral renaissance (Flexner, 1975).

At the turn of the twentieth century, more and more Americans experienced the devastating impact of a manufacturing-based economy controlled by corporate interests. Economic depression and worker uprisings inspired a new breed of activism, shaped, as before, by the interests and sympathies of mothers and wives. Jane Addams, dissatisfied with social Darwinism's victim-blaming explanations of poverty, organized the Settlement House movement, effectively adapting women's family-based domesticity to broader social needs.[6] Hull House in Chicago was the most famous settlement house in the United States. Committed to improving the quality of life of the urban poor, Addams and the workers and volunteers at Hull House rallied working-class Chicagoans, especially women and children employed in sweatshops, to organize for better working conditions and pay. Addams, like her contemporaries in the female moral reform movement, believed that it was "stupid . . . to permit the mothers of young children to spend themselves in the coarser work of the world" (quoted in Wilson, 1991, p. 73).

Another outlet for women activists was local-level club activity, gathered under the umbrella of the General Federation of Women's Clubs (GFWC). The GFWC emerged as the "secular equivalent of the WCTU" and the "chief voice of organized womanhood after 1910" (Sklar, 1993, p. 63). Within these clubs, women realized a progressive vision that combined gender consciousness with an awareness of class-based injustice. In fact, Sklar argues, "women's organizational heyday between 1880 and 1930 brought a new and vital constituency into American political life at a time when women's political perspectives and resources were urgently needed" (1993, p. 77).[7] Maternalist politics manifested itself in the United States in an variety of ways, including the growth of care-taking professions for women, such as social work and nursing (Koven and Michel, 1993).[8]

In this era, middle-class women shaped visions of social reform, bringing attention to the needs of poor women and their children.[9] Seth Koven and Sonya Michel (1993) attribute the gains made to the social acceptability of the maternalist agenda, and the losses to the political climate of the time. For instance, female social reformers favored protective legislation dictating hours, wages, and working conditions for women and children. Once enacted, laws conceived to help women effectively blocked them from the workplace, limiting their earnings and bolstering the dual labor market (Koven and Michel, 1993, p. 18).[10]

Mother's pensions were another goal of female reformers during the Progressive era. The GFWC combined forces with the National Congress of Mothers (NCM), the WCTU, and other groups in a state-by-state campaign to establish public funding for mothers deprived of a male breadwinner. The advocates invoked characteristically maternalist rhetoric, arguing that such pensions sustained the mother–child bond. Mrs. Frederic Schoff, president of the NCM and the Parent-Teacher Association, invited mothers to "build a bridge upon which struggling humanity may safely cross into a new land, leaving forever the old, with its unending reformatory movements, its shattered homes; and the keystone of that bridge will be maternal love, while in that fair domain the splendid edifice of the new civilization will bear the cornerstone of home" (quoted in Michel, 1993, pp. 296–97).

Clubwomen worked hard to distinguish mother's pensions from the charity payments of earlier days, portraying the pensions as a salary for the *work* of mothering. Mothering had a civic value: Mothers, after all, produced citizens and soldiers and should be compensated for their labor. But, they argued, pensions should be provided only to women deprived of male support, thereby codifying the ideology of women's dependence on men and the family wage (Michel, 1993).

Still another project associated with Progressive era female reformers was the day nursery movement. Maternalists pushed for public funding of childcare for wage-earning mothers, but without success. As Michel (1993, pp. 281–90) shows, the same maternalist discourses grounded in traditional white, middle-class conceptions of women's familial roles that succeeded in enacting mothers' pensions defeated the day nursery movement. The maternalists' limited vision of women's rights and responsibilities—one that codified gender difference—was compatible with a program that kept women in the home but not with one that supported women as wage-earners.[11]

By World War I, cracks and splits were evident in the women's reform movement. Passage of the Equal Rights Amendment was a key point of division. The National Women's Suffrage Association (NWSA) represented the radical view, which stressed women's equality and advocated structural reforms in government, education, and labor (see Flexner, 1975). More moderate activists concentrated their efforts on the passage of the Sheppard-Towner Maternal and Child Health Bill, which provided federal matching grants to the states for information and instruction on nutrition and hygiene, prenatal and child-health clinics, and visiting nurses for pregnant women and new mothers (Ladd-Taylor, 1993, p. 322). The bill was ultimately defeated in Congress in 1929 (Ryan, 1983), the year the stock market crashed.

Women responded to the economic crisis by scraping up whatever wages they could in the paid workforce and by reviving home-based production to mitigate the family's loss of wages. Curiously, the ideology of separate spheres grew stronger during this period, and women merely added paid labor to the myriad forms of unpaid labor they already performed. Born of necessity and desperation, this development may have left many women with a negative view of work outside the home (Milkman, 1979, in Ginsberg, 1989, p. 241). Although the Depression temporarily weakened the *practice of* domesticity as women's solitary enterprise (for more privileged women), the *ideology* of domesticity gained force.

*practice slightly weathened,
~~to do~~ ideology gained force.*

During World War II and its aftermath, female reform activity waned, but not its ideological basis, domesticity. Although significant numbers of women who had been pulled into the wartime labor force remained in lower-paying, lower-skilled service jobs (Milkman, 1979, p. 529), the ideology of woman's-place-in-the-home prevailed. The sacred mother of the Victorian era was back, but this time her confidence was undermined by a popular science that presumed to know more about rearing children than mothers themselves. A plethora of "experts" dictated how best to rear baby, prescribing complicated and rigid procedures and intensive mother–baby togetherness (see Thurer, 1994). But what accounts for this revival of domesticity? Elaine Tyler May (1988) argues that the self-contained home, sexually charged, isolated, and characterized by abundance, offered security in the shadow of nuclear threat. The American family attempted to meet every member's needs through family life, although few succeeded.[12] According to May, the domestic ideology dominant in this era fostered the very tendencies it regarded as the perils of the times: materialism, consumerism, and bureaucratic conformity. This ideology of the self-contained home kept Communism and other mysterious and feared social forces at bay and quelled grass-roots activism.

When the children of post–World War II families came of age, activism was rejuvenated. Some of the most visible of this new breed of activists were second-wave feminists who denounced women's domesticity, and especially motherhood, as the basis of women's oppression. Other feminists rallied for equal pay for equal work and supported the commodification of the domestic sphere (through paid childcare and maid service, for example) to free women from their domestic prisons (see Freeman, 1979).[13] There were limits to these tactics, however. A feminist preoccupation with motherhood and domesticity reduced women's identity to its reproductive function: "As the material base of domesticity has been subsumed into the market economy, female identity is increasingly defined by and reduced to reproduction" (Ginsberg, 1989, p. 247).

This struggle over identity manifests itself in the contemporary abortion debate. Antiabortion activists resemble female moral reformers of the past two hundred years who subscribed to a woman-as-different ideology, believing that women embody a uniquely feminine constellation of qualities, including nurturance and sensitivity. Convinced that materialism and narcissism are unraveling society, they call for a return to nurturance, kin, and community and see it as their (often God-given) duty to reverse the devaluation of women's essential being (Ginsberg, 1989, p. 7).

At the start of the twenty-first century, female moral reform continues in a new guise. Like their predecessors, today's maternalists embrace the notion that an essential female nature shapes the practices of motherhood and a larger female reality. (Some oppose abortion, and some do not.) This position has certain theoretical and political limits.

The assumption that there are essential differences between men and women guided the maternalist discourses and strategies of moral reformers throughout American history. In the language of the eighteenth century, women were "chosen vessels" endowed with a piety and morality that protected them from the dehumanizing effects of commercial capitalism and uniquely prepared them to nurture the family and purify society. As the Industrial Age progressed, more secular interpretations of women's essence prevailed, most notably the "cult of true womanhood." To survive their changing circumstances, Epstein argues, it was necessary for women to internalize male dominance, "rather than simply obey men out of fear of withdrawal of economic support or the sanctions of the law" (1981, p. 81). As a direct result, any chance of gender equity was undermined. In Cott's view, women faced the cruel irony of creating the very thing that destroyed their self-determination (1977, pp. 197–206).

Historians debate the extent of women's agency in this system. Some, like Ryan (1981), argue that women at least enjoyed authority in the household and, later, in the polity as shapers of a limited range of public policy. Others, like Epstein, argue that the ideology of separate spheres "made it more difficult for [women] to criticize a family structure and moral code that forced women into restricted roles" (1981, p. 149). Based on the historical evidence summarized here, I contend that notions of gender difference, whether seen as divinely or naturally derived, serve to concretize gender inequality. The authority women "enjoy" in the home operates as an illusion of power and self-determination or, in Foucauldian terms, a form of the "invisible" internalized power of the state (Foucault, 1995). Because women "buy into" this logic, enforcement (by men, institutions, or both) is rendered virtually unnecessary; women police themselves as good mothers and good wives who protect the socially constructed boundary between women and men. At best, female moral reform presents a paradox: Maternalism may have achieved some gains for women and children, but it simultaneously reinforced the male-dominated status quo. Maternalist discourses have offered not a politics of transformation, but one of accommodation.

Today's natural mothers are, I argue, a contemporary variant of the female moral reformers and embrace a similar politics of accommodation. While they resist certain capitalist structures and attempt to wrest control from institutions and challenge "experts" they perceive as threatening to the best interests of American families, they do not challenge the structure and content of gender relations. Their revolutionary project is to model the valuation of female productivity in the interest of cultivating a gentler, less material, more family-centered social climate. Although the natural mothers may enjoy some success in this arena, I argue that their efforts have another, perhaps unintended, consequence—an adaptation to patriarchal notions about women and men, including the gendered division of labor and, more abstractly, the dualistic split between private and public spheres and the exaltation of biology as the shaper of human destiny. I develop this critique in more depth in Chapters 4 through 6.

comments from the 5 mothers

MORE comments from the 5 mothers:

"Sequencing" - women can have it all, but not at once.

"Knowing," "Felt Right", "intuition" - all these things are mentioned by the natural mothers, but yet their approach to mothering is at odds w/ mainstream culture.

32. The contradictory nature of natural mothering as a social movement.

33. The route to natural mothering is different for each mother, yet certain themes serve as common markers along the varied themes paths.

Female moral reform : (note to

35. The thread of female moral reform runs through American history from the late 18th century to the present - as the author argues - "natural mothering" is a part of this reform movement.

36. Domesticity brought material comfort, refuge from the perplexing economic world, and perplexing economic world - A mixed blessing

37. motherhood (1800's) was further santified in an emerging ideology called as "cult of true womenhood". (Thought to be incompatible with the "outside world") Their virtues piety, purity, submissiveness, and domesticity. (women did embrace this)

38. The arena of morality "women's sphere", a distinct privileged status and

3 A Closer Look

41. Womens organizational hey day between 1880-1930.

The Ideological Components of Natural Mothering

73. Although the practice of domesticity, domesticity was temporarily weakened by the depression, the ideology gained force.
    disputed the
first WAVE Feminists: cult of domesticity, and especially motherhood
second   as the basis of women's oppression; others supported childcare

Natural mothering merges two lifestyle practices—Voluntary Simplicity and Attachment Parenting—while taking inspiration from Cultural Feminism (Figure 1). All three elements are closely intertwined, but I will attempt to disentangle these sometimes uneasy partners to demonstrate the most significant constitutive elements of natural mothering.

Voluntary Simplicity: An Attempt at Lifestyle Revolution

Conserving resources at home and taking on economic and political issues are as inseparable as the yolk and white of a scrambled egg. It never works to say, "I'll stop using paper towels and driving a big car, but I won't take this world hunger thing past my own door post." Once an egg yolk breaks into the white, there's no way to remove every tiny gold fleck. Just so, once you walk into a supermarket or pull up to a gas pump, you are part of the economic and political sphere. Certainly your influence is small. But whether you conserve or waste, it is real. Many people using or not using affects things in a big way. Gathering up the fragments of our waste—recycling, conserving, sharing—is a logical and authentic beginning. Such actions are the first fruits of the harvest of justice. They are the promise of more to come.

—Doris Janzen Longacre, *Living More with Less* (1981, p. 27)

48

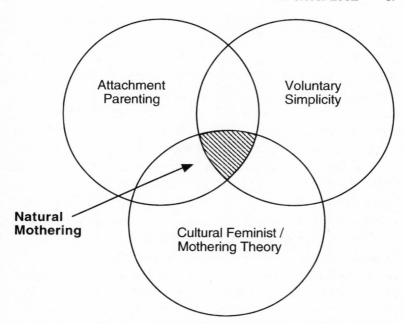

Figure I. The constitutive elements of natural mothering.

Voluntary Simplicity (VS), also known as Simple Living, dictates a lifestyle that derives meaning from relative austerity and minimized consumption. As Doris Longacre suggests, VS is predicated on the belief that individual well-being is entangled with the well-being of society at large. Proponents live frugally, rejecting material preoccupations and opting for recycling, bartering, and trading in place of traditional market exchange. They seek meaning in "doing it oneself," freed from the constraints of institutions and experts who claim to know best.

The term "Voluntary Simplicity" was coined in 1936 by Richard Gregg, a student of Gandhi, and the practice spread quietly among a diffuse group of individuals until a small but loyal hippie population picked up on the idea in the 1970s (Elgin, 1993, p. 24). In 1981 the movement garnered wider attention when Duane Elgin wrote a book entitled, not surprisingly, *Voluntary Simplicity: Living a Life That Is Outwardly Simple and Inwardly Rich*. Re-released in 1993, it explored in depth what Elgin labeled "living on the new frontier" (p. 21): "In the last several decades, a growing number of people have been exploring a simpler way of life. Without major media coverage to mark its progress, the growth in simpler ways of living has emerged largely unnoticed in many developed nations. Quietly and without fanfare people have been developing ways of living that touch the world more lightly and compassionately" (1993, p. 57).

Elgin characterizes the people who undertook the experiment of Simple Living as pioneers who "stand with a foot in two worlds—with one foot in an unraveling industrial civilization and another foot in a newly arising post-civilization." These "in-betweeners," as he calls them, are creating an amalgam of the old and the new that brings both practical and spiritual meaning to life: "Simplicity of living is being driven both by the push of necessity (the need to find more sustainable ways to live) and the pull of opportunity (the realistic possibility of finding more satisfying ways to live)" (p. 37).

Simplicity is catching on. A 1994 report by the Trends Research Institute, a New York–based independent research group, estimated that approximately 4 percent of the 77 million American baby boomers (about 3.1 million people) have adopted simpler lives. By the year 2002 that number may swell to 15 percent of baby boomers. Gerald Celente of the Trends Research Institute attributes the trend primarily to the harsh economic realities of the early 1990s, without addressing either the corporate reorganizations at the root of these realities or the fact that the 1990s were a boom time for many. Many simplifiers were forced to reconstruct their lifestyles as a result of corporate downsizing; others, he says, are "retro hippies" who "want to return to the ideals they had during the Woodstock era" (Knight-Ridder, 1996). Three years later, Celente remained focused on simplicity. His 1997 book *Trends 2000* (a *Wall Street Journal* bestseller) lists Voluntary Simplicity as one of the top trends of the twenty-first century (Celente, 1997; see especially pp. 161–76).

Linda Breen Pierce, principal investigator of the Pierce Simplicity Study, an independent web-based research project, argues that simplicity proponents enjoy a deep connection with nature. Drawing on qualitative data collected via an internet questionnaire (an irony not lost on Pierce) and follow-up phone interviews, she found a committed environmental awareness at the root of most simplicity practice (Pierce, 2000).

Juliet Schor, the Harvard economist perhaps best known for her book *The Overworked American* (1992), has turned her attention to VS as well. In *The Overspent American* (1998), Schor concerns herself with the myriad forces that compel contemporary Americans to spend beyond their means, asking why Americans retain their penchant for conspicuous consumerism even when doing so takes a toll on familial relationships, long-term financial security, and quality of life in general. In a chapter devoted to "The Downshifter Next Door," she profiles people who have voluntarily or involuntarily cut back their incomes and, accordingly, their spending. Schor presents statistical data derived from 800 telephone interviews with randomly chosen adults nationwide. Conducted by EDK Associates, Inc., of New York, the survey revealed that a full 28 percent of respondents identified themselves as "voluntary downshifters." Schor herself interviewed 27 individuals who had undergone either voluntary or involuntary downshifts. She resists characterizing members of the VS movement based on her small sample, but she sees "certain demographic features" as "salient" (1998, p. 136).

According to Schor, proponents of Simple Living tend to be middle-class, white, and at least college-educated; they are more likely to be women than men and unlikely to have young children living at home. They are more likely to be single than married and tend be "a bit older" (presumably meaning older than the mean age of the U.S. population). Schor is careful to differentiate between downshifters and simple livers. The key difference, she contends, is that downshifters make a trade-off between time and money, deciding that their time is more valuable than their income and that they will therefore live with less. Simple livers, by contrast, "transcend that trade-off" (1998, p. 138). They establish a maximum level of income beyond which it is unacceptable to live. Spending beyond this determined level is immoral for some, environmentally insensitive, alienating, wrong-headed, or clutter-inducing for others. For them, less is truly more.

Whatever leads people to practice simplicity, it is clear that growing numbers of people are attracted to the idea. The newsletter *Simple Living*, founded in 1992, attracted over twenty-five hundred subscribers in its first three years of existence (Brophy, 1995, p. 96). Its founder, Janet Luhrs, upon finishing her law degree, decided that she would rather stay at home with her young children than begin practicing law at once. Soon thereafter, she launched *Simple Living*. While standing in line at the grocery store, it is not unusual to spot the word "simplicity" in a headline in a popular magazine. The glossy *Simplycity* (subtitled "Ideas, style, euphoria, home, frivolities") and *Real Simple*, which premiered in April 2000, are on the newsstands. Clearly, simplicity is marketable, and this was apparent even in the mid-1990s. The cover of *Self*'s December 1996 issue, emblazoned "The Simple Life: How You Can Get It," promised "92 Ideas to Relieve Stress, Reduce Clutter, Save Time and Clear Your Mind." *Prevention*'s September 1997 issue urged: "Simplify Your Life (And *Finally* Have Free Time)." *Ladies' Home Journal* (April 1997) jumped on the simplicity bandwagon with "8 Mind-Body Tactics to Stop Stress, Slow Down, Simplify." *Cooking Light*'s "Special Holiday Issue" for 1996 featured the words "Simplify Your Holidays" against a photograph of "Easy Chocolate-Caramel Brownies." Even the fashion world has appropriated the growing appeal of the Simple Living trend: The *Milwaukee Journal Sentinel* ran a story under a front-page preview headline that Voluntary Simplifiers would see as most ironic: "The News for Spring Fashion Is Simplicity" (Fitzpatrick, 1997).

A recent bibliographic search for books related to simple living produced 125 titles (the earliest dating to 1904); 88 of these (70 percent) were published in the 1990s. Elaine St. James's works may be the most ubiquitous. Her *Simplify Your Life: 100 Ways to Slow Down and Really Enjoy the Things That Matter* (1994) was released in a gift edition in time for the 1997 winter holidays. Her *Inner Simplicity* (1995) has 386,000 copies in print; *Simplify Life with Your Kids* (2000) is addressed to busy parents who reject prescriptions for Simple Living as impossible for families busy with softball practice, PTA meetings, and mounds of laundry. (Paradoxically, Hyperion, her publisher, is a subsidiary of Disney.) Other popular titles include Doris Janzen Longacre's *Living More with Less* (1981), written from a Mennonite perspective, and Joe Dominguez and Vicki Robin's *Your Money or Your Life* (1992). Some cast (the late) Dominguez and Robin as the gurus of the VS movement (see Brophy, 1995; Schor, 1995). Their book sold 350,000 copies in its first three years in print, grossing $3.5 million dollars for its publisher; to date, it has sold more than 700,000 copies (see the website www.newroadmap.org). Sue Bender's *Plain and Simple: A Woman's Journey to the Amish* (1989), Amy Dacyczn's *The Complete Tightwad Gazette* (1999), and Scott and Helen Nearing's *The Good Life* (1990) are other popular examples of this genre. The *Simple Living* newsletter's founder and editor Janet Luhrs published in 1997 perhaps the most complete text, *The Simple Living Guide,* a 444-page volume whose dust jacket proclaims it to be the definitive VS resource and "a source book for less stressful, more joyful living." Some of the natural mothers I interviewed had read a number of the books mentioned above; others had not, explaining to me the difficulty of obtaining them at their local library. Several shook their heads in disgust when the ever-growing market for simplicity books came up in our discussions. VS, for them, is a noble and worthy enterprise that is compromised when opportunists (with dubious allegiance to VS) appropriate the concept to sell more books.

A video entitled *Affluenza,* produced jointly by a Seattle television station and Oregon Public Broadcasting and narrated by National Public Radio's Scott Simon, aired nationally on PBS in prime time in fall 1997; it has since been made available for purchase. On the package, the video is characterized as "a fascinating look at one of the greatest social maladies of our time: overconsumption and materialism." Implicating "swollen expectations, hypercommercialism, shopping fever, a rash of bankruptcies, fractured families, chronic stress, social scars and resource exhaustion" as the symptoms of "affluenza," the program prescribes VS as "just one of many cures" (de Graaf and Boe, 1997). On the

Affluenza Project's website, Jessie O'Neill's book *The Golden Ghetto: The Psychology of Affluence* (1997) is aggressively marketed to visitors who wish to learn more about this so-called "national epidemic." The internet has emerged as a treasure trove of information on VS. An early site was the Northwest Earth Institute's Voluntary Simplicity Discussion Group, which provides a curriculum for organizing local groups. "The Simple Living Network" is "specifically tailored for those looking to craft a healthier, more meaningful lifestyle" (SNL website [www.simpleliving.net], 2001). It provides an extensive web-based resource center featuring various products available to consumers "interested in changing their patterns of consumption" (SLN website, 2001). Recognizing the irony of such a business venture, the founders admit that "we struggle daily with the issue of whether or not we should be in business at all" (SLN website, 2001).

Seattle is in fact the epicenter of the movement. Cecile Andrews writes a weekly column for the *Seattle Times* titled "Voluntary Simplicity" and at one time co-hosted a radio show called "Simple Living" for KUOW, an NPR affiliate in Seattle. Andrews published *The Circle of Simplicity: Return to the Good Life* in 1997.

American advertising recognizes a hot trend when it sees one. The other day a membership solicitation from Columbia House's CD club arrived in my mail with the words "Simplify Your Life" emblazoned at the top. Liberty Check Company markets direct deposit with the very same words, run underneath a photograph of a person relaxing in a hammock stretched between two lovely palm trees. California Closets uses the same trusted phrase in its magazine ad depicting a home office. The furniture manufacturer Techline uses a variation on the theme, "This is Simplicity," in a direct-mail campaign. Ethan Allen ran a full page ad in the *New York*

Times (September 10, 2000) showcasing a pine bed and nightstand with the words, "Simplify—Where Less is Clearly More." Nordstrom's simplicity-themed ad in the same paper (November 14, 1999) depicted a completely empty and illuminated three-car garage with a full dumpster within view nearby. "Make room for shoes," the text advises. But perhaps the most notable example of the appropriation of simplicity by savvy marketers is Honda's handiwork.

In 1997 Honda launched an advertising campaign suggesting that in a world of overwhelming options, the sanest, wisest, most reasonable choice is the simplest one—the purchase of a Honda. The print version of the ad occupied two pages. On the first page, the reader confronted a dizzying array of finely differentiated choices (of hot sauces or men's haircuts). The text read: "Life is full of complicated decisions." The next page depicted one of Honda's models with a single word centered on the page: "Simplify." In the television ad, a woman stood before a cluttered closet. Shoes, belts, pants, dresses, purses, filled every bit of her closet space. Suddenly, the closet began to tip, and its contents spilled out. The woman held on to the clothing bar for dear life as the room continued to tilt and her possessions tumbled out of the closet. Finally, the room righted itself—empty now—and a car pulled up before the puzzled woman. "Simplify" appeared on the screen.

Proctor & Gamble adopted a new "strategy of simplification" because, according to president and chief operating officer Durk Jager, "It's mind boggling how difficult we've made it for consumers over the years." Believing that consumers are overwhelmed by too many choices on their drug and grocery store shelves, P & G decided to pare back its product roster and concentrate its marketing efforts on a few basic brands. As a result, P & G's market share in hair care alone grew to nearly 36.5 percent from 1991 to 1996. Other companies are adopting what *Business Week* dubbed P & G's "marketing mantra": Nabisco, Toyota, Citibank, Clorox, General Motors, Colgate-Palmolive, and Kraft streamlined their own product lines, development costs, and advertising budgets (*Business Week,* September 1996, p. 98).

The unlikely bedmates of corporate America and contemporary simplifiers may believe that they have discovered a new trend, but Simple Living is not new at all. Simplicity as a moral imperative has periodically emerged throughout American history. In *The Simple Life: Plain Living and High Thinking in American Culture* (1985), David Shi documents the numerous forms a preference for Simple Living has taken over time. They share a common ideology: the idea that "the making of money and the accumulation of things should not smother the purity of the soul, the life of the mind, the cohesion of the family, or the good of the commonwealth" (1985, p. 3).[1] Beginning with the Puritans and Quakers and following the theme into a contemporary age challenged by "affluence and anxiety," Shi demonstrates not only the different manifestations of Simple Living (and their historical contexts) but also the persistent core assumptions that translate into everyday practice. And that practice, Shi finds, differs for women and men: "Men may have been the most prominent spokesmen for the ethic, but women have most often been responsible for translating the ideal into domestic practice" (p. 65). For example, Shi recounts the experience of the women at Fruitlands, a communal living experiment conducted in Harvard, Massachusetts, in the mid-1840s and associated with Transcendentalism. "There was only one slave at Fruitlands, . . . and that was a woman," Abigail Alcott, the wife of Fruitlands' founder, wrote in her diary (Shi, 1985, p. 137). Abigail's daughter,

Louisa May, recalled that the men of Fruitlands "were so busy discussing and defining great duties that they forgot to perform the small ones" (p. 137). Abigail herself recorded a remark made by another Fruitlander that perhaps best expressed her own frustration: "Miss Page made a good remark, and as true as good," Alcott wrote in her journal, "that a woman may live a whole life of sacrifice and at her death meekly say, 'I die a woman.' But a man passes with a few years in experiments in self-denial and simple life, and he says, 'Behold, I am a God'" (p. 138).

Alcott's observations bring to mind a series of questions related to the division of labor and the practice of Voluntary Simplicity. Does the commitment to Simple Living vary by gender, or, alternatively, is the obligation to put it into practice gendered? Or, perhaps, is it "natural" for women to perform most of the actual work necessary in the simplified life because Voluntary Simplicity is actually dependent on the creation of surplus value, for which women are famously responsible? Shi's intellectual history suggests that the connection is not coincidental. At the turn of the twentieth century, he argues, Simple Living was tied to the emerging cult of true womanhood, which some historians regard as a concerted attempt by American men to "shift the bulk of their moral burden to the shoulder of women" (Shi, 1985, p. 11), and others as a strategy to keep women in the home, far from the burgeoning women's rights movement.

Some see VS as marking the beginning of a tide of change with which we must reckon. Gerald Celente of the Trends Research Institute calls it "the most significant lifestyle change since the Depression" (Knight-Ridder, 1996): "We are at the beginning of a socioeconomic transition that will be at least as great as the transition from an agrarian society to an industrial society. Down scaled lifestyles will be a key element of a new way of life that people are inventing now," he claims (Guidera, 1995).

Nonetheless, scholars, with a few exceptions, have shown little interest in VS to date. Avraham Shama and Joe Wisenblit provide a psychological profile of practitioners, finding that "values of Voluntary Simplicity and behaviors are consistent [with each other and] the motivation for Voluntary Simplicity includes personal preference and economic hardship" (1984, p. 231).[2] For example, strongly held VS values such as ecological responsibility and "small is beautiful" are typically associated with such practices as bartering, recycling, and composting (pp. 236–37). In an expanded study that looked at VS values and practices in three cities, Shama (1988) found consistent responses in all three. T. P. Nolen's 1994 dissertation at the University of North Carolina-Greensboro examines the factors that lead individuals to adopt simpler lives, the meaning of VS, the ways in which it is practiced, and, finally, the role of group support in the pursuit of Simple Living. In general, Nolen found that while ethical issues were more important motivations than ecological or economic concerns, once people began the simplification process they increasingly placed environmental concerns foremost.

In an article entitled "Why (and How) More People are Dropping Out of the Rat Race," Juliet Schor observes that "complaints about excessive consumerism were rampant in the '80s, but lately people seem to be rejecting the 'I shop, therefore I am' credo in deed as well as word" (1995, p. 14). Citing a Merck Family Fund poll, Schor suggests that "women are at the forefront" of this anticonsumerism trend: 75 percent of American men feel that Americans buy more than they need, but 89 percent of women think so. Schor's own poll, conducted at one of the nation's largest telecom companies, found that 83 percent of men and 88 percent of women agree with the statement "Americans are too materialistic" (p. 14).

Sorting out how many people actually change their patterns of consumption in accordance with their values is another matter, and one that poses problems for researchers. People may admit that excessive consumption is a problem, but saying so does not necessarily mean that simplification is a value or a targeted behavior. Some individuals do report lifestyle changes—for instance, the Merck Poll found that 32 percent of women and 23.5 percent of men reported "downshifting" (defined as taking a lower-paying job to reduce hours or quitting work outside the home altogether). What is unclear from these data is the economic, familial, cultural, and social context in which individuals choose to "downshift." Clearly, more research is needed into Voluntary Simplicity, its adherents, and the multidimensional context in which it is situated.

Attachment Parenting

Attachment parenting (AP) is many many things. Mostly, it is an attitude that involves listening closely and responding to your babies/children's needs. It is about responding when a baby cries and disciplining without spanking. It is about being available to your children. It is a belief that when a baby cries it is trying to communicate to you and that it is your job to figure out what he/she needs. It is about forming strong bonds when they are young and allowing them to move away and become independent at their own pace. That is the heart of AP.
        —On-line Parent-L discussion list

A substantial subset of natural mothers adhere to the principles of Attachment Parenting (AP), the second component of natural mothering. Although Voluntary Simplicity can be practiced by anyone dissatisfied with mainstream cultural prescriptions about how to live a meaningful life, AP addresses the specific concerns of *parents* who seek to depart from what they believe is the norm in a changing, alienating, and child-decentered culture. Like Simple Living, "parenting differently" is not a new practice, but a very old one. In the mid-1970s, the self-trained anthropologist Jean Liedloff reintroduced old world parenting to new world, Western parents. In *The Continuum Concept* (1985), she describes her fieldwork with South American Indians, children and mothers whom she describes as calm and well-adjusted. Drawing on this experience, she conceived the "continuum concept"—"the chain of experience of our species which is suited to the tendencies and expectations which we have evolved" (1985, pp. 22–23). Basically, "continuum babies" are parented like the babies Liedloff observed in South America. They are held constantly by the mother (or, when absolutely necessary, by others) and nursed on demand; they sleep with the mother. Liedloff argues that babies have expectations that must be met if they are to mature into healthy, productive, and happy children and adults. The key to this development is constant mother–baby contact at least until the baby learns to crawl. Any other approach to childrearing denies the baby's innate needs.[3]

In the late 1980s William and Martha Sears, a family practice physician and his wife, a nurse, coined the term "Attachment Parenting." Although they do not refer to Liedloff's work, the similarity in their ideas is striking. AP, the Sears argue in their series of popular and widely available books on pregnancy, birth, infancy, toddlerhood, and discipline, is the best way to create and maintain a bond with your children. It facilitates healthy physical, spiritual, emotional, and moral child development by placing a premium on extended mother–child physical contact: "This style is a way of caring that brings out the best in parents and their babies. Attachment parenting has been around as long as there have been mothers and babies. It is, in fact, only recently that this style of parenting has needed a name at all, for it is basically common sense parenting we all would do if left to our own healthy resources" (Sears and Sears, 1993, p. 2). The five "tools" of AP are: (1) connect with your baby early; (2) read and respond to your baby's cues; (3) wear your baby (i.e., carry him or her close to your body as much as possible, preferably using a "baby sling"; (4) breastfeed your baby; (5) share sleep with your baby (p. 5).

Although AP's commonsense approach to childrearing seems humane, the link between such practices and the outcomes predicted by AP advocates are unproven. Moreover, questions about its feasibility remain. What happens when real mothers and fathers make the sacrifices necessary to reject aids such as bottles, pacifiers, strollers, and cribs? What happens when the mother must go to work outside the home? What does it cost to enact a lifestyle in which the child is "at the center of the universe"? What kind of child does this lifestyle produce? At this point, no studies have tested AP's effect on child development and mother–child bonding, but anecdotal evidence abounds. In my own small-scale study of La Leche League members, many women reluctantly acknowledged the costs of consistently and repeatedly subordinating their own needs to those of their children. One informant explained: "I remember putting my needs way last, and after three years I had such a deficit in meeting my needs, all I wanted to say was, 'No. No. No. No. No'" (Bobel, 2001).

Perhaps one of the greatest risks of the daily application of AP is the guilt that results when mothers fail to live up to the expectations created by the philosophy. Compounding this guilt is the fear that the mother who "fails" to attach properly to her baby is somehow not woman enough—if she were, she could easily perform tasks that purportedly "come naturally." As Marjorie DeVault argues:

> Discourses of "family life"—instructions for being a "wife" and especially for "mothering"—suggest that those for whom the models are often inappropriate should be held to the same standards as others, and if they do not measure up, should be blamed, as inadequate women, for their families' difficulties. By locating the blame on individuals rather than structures, these discourses legitimate the hierarchies of access to resources that produce inequities. (1991, p. 230)

This critique of AP is reminiscent of a popular criticism of the "new age" and holistic health movements (the health care choice for most natural mothers). Kristin Alster may have put it best:

> Too much emphasis has been placed in the movement on what individuals can and should do for themselves and too little on what they can expect from professional care providers. There is also little recognition of the limits of personal endeavor and will power. Expectations have been created that cannot be met, and when they are not, much unhappiness results. (1989, p. 134)

AP remains a powerful force shaping the day-to-day reality of natural mothers, and like Voluntary Simplicity it shows signs of gaining broader popular appeal. For instance, a recent internet search turned up websites like the Natural Child Project, described as a resource providing "advice and articles on parenting and education that respects children," the Calgary-based Whole Family Parenting Association, the

Natural Family Site, Families for Natural Living.org, the Muslim Attachment Parenting Page, and Christian Families for Natural Living.org. In addition to these information and support sites, there exist a plethora of sites peddling products for the attached and/or natural family. All-natural skin products, cloth diaper wraps, baby slings (cloth carriers), books, crafts, and more are for sale on sites like natureandnurture.com and mothersnature.com.

When I began studying Attachment Parenting in 1994, only a handful of sites matched those key words. A recent search produced no fewer than 82,300 hits. (A more advanced search generated 5,130.) The growing number of cyber-based AP resources suggests that a community may be taking shape. Parentsplace, an interactive internet community, offers hundreds of services to participants, including chat boards, bulletin boards, and an online newsletter supportive of Attachment Parenting. A number of discussion lists operate as a more intimate forum. Founded in 1994 and boasting an international membership, "Parent-L" identifies itself as a list for parents who support extended breastfeeding and Attachment Parenting. "Rad Mamas" was created as the radical alternative to what some members considered the increasingly mainstream Parent-L. The fact that some mothers regarded Parent-L as too conventional offers perhaps the best evidence of AP's widening appeal.

A growing number of print resources promote and support AP. The Winter 1995 issue of the *Nurturing Parent*, an "international journal to encourage healthy parent–child relationships through Attachment Parenting Practices," includes articles on "The Continuum Kitchen," "The Family Bed: Dispelling the Myths," and the "Rhythm of Homeschooling." *Informed Alternatives in Parenting* promises to "[help] parents make the most informed childrearing decisions." The November 1995 issue features articles such as "Cuddle While You Can," "The End of Daycare Blues" (written by an at-home dad), and "Reflections on Love and Attachment," contributed by a clinical psychologist. Perhaps the best-known and most widely circulated AP periodical is *Mothering* (recently subtitled "the Magazine of Natural Family Living"). Founded in the 1970s by current editor-in-chief Peggy O'Mara, *Mothering* claims an international readership of 205,660. Informational sections include "The Art of Mothering," "Health," "Pregnancy, Birth and Midwifery," "Ways of Learning," and "Family Living." *Mothering* has changed from a radical magazine on newsprint to a glossy, smartly designed periodical; some long-time readers (including many of the natural mothers I spoke with) complain that it has lost its radical edge. After it sold advertising space to a national disposable diaper delivery service (see the Spring 1995 issue), floods of angry letters accused the magazine of "selling out" to "mass-market culture." "Where is the voice of alternative motherhood if not in *Mothering*?" some readers asked (see Summer 1995, pp. 11–12, and Fall 1995, pp. 9–11).

Not long after, *Mothering* published a special issue devoted to "the vaccination question" (June 1996). To the dismay of many readers (including, again, many in my sample), the issue contained more material in support of vaccination than against it. Again, some loyal readers concluded that *Mothering* had blunted its edge to accommodate a wider range of readers who may not subscribe to the most radical features of AP and natural living. These developments suggest that AP and, more broadly, the natural family living the magazine promotes, may be spreading beyond the original "fringe" cohort. And they raise a question: Does the editorial shift of *Mothering* suggest a cooptation of both movements, much like the advertising industry's appropriation of the public's growing fascination with Simple Living? Does the diluted content of *Mothering* mean that a particular lifestyle once practiced by certain "hippie" moms is now gaining popularity among more mainstream mothers, or do dilution and wider accessibility merely tell us that Simple Living and AP "sell"?

Standing its ground, *Compleat Mother* is still printed on newsprint, features very explicit images of breastfeeding mothers and children, and is designed in an unapologetically homespun style, all the aesthetic and editorial hallmarks of outsider status. "Mother," as its readers call it, addresses pregnancy, birth, and breastfeeding issues. Its mission is to provide affirmation to women who give birth at home, nurse their children well beyond toddlerhood, share the family bed, and engage in other alternative parenting practices. It is for women "who act alone but need not feel alone."

A growing attachment industry parallels the one spawned, ironically, by Simple Living. Each week, it seems, my own mailbox is graced by the catalog of yet another attachment-style or natural living mail order operation: "The Natural Baby Catalog," "Doctor Possum," "Babyworks." Some, like "Doctor Possum," concentrate on natural care products, while others, like "Back to Basics," promote simple (and often "throwback") toys purportedly designed to encourage gentle, noncompetitive play. A number of catalogs sell baby slings in every fabric and style, derived from nearly every developing country—the *only* piece of "baby equipment" many attachment parents claim a family needs. Devices designed for nursing mothers include a special foot stool, nursing pillows, and nipple creams. A plethora of book catalogs (among them "Chinaberry," "Natural Resources," and "Whole Child") list titles congruent with AP theory and practice. A burgeoning nursing-wear mail order market was pioneered by "Motherwear," whose catalog periodically offers a pull-out mini-magazine featuring articles and editorials in support of natural living, extended breastfeeding, and Attachment Parenting.[4]

Cultural Feminist and Mothering Theories: Celebrating the Uniqueness of Woman

> Liberal feminists believe women should paint oils like men and hang them next to men's paintings in great museums. Cultural feminists believe women should display their quilts.
> —Barbara Katz Rothman, lecture, 1996

Whereas the preceding sections demonstrated the practical components of natural mothering, we will now explore natural mothering as an outgrowth of cultural feminist theory. In the late 1970s, a strain of feminist theory reemerged that recalled some first-wave cultural feminist approaches to women's liberation—the ones that focused on the unique characteristics of women.

Unlike the "cult of true womanhood" (Welter, 1976), which defined women as pure, pious, domestic, and submissive and was specific to privileged white women during the Jacksonian period in the United States, current cultural feminist approaches distinguish women from men by focusing on women as nurturing, intuitive, and relationship-oriented, regardless of class or race. Past or present, cultural feminist theory celebrates women's presumed essential qualities—a approach that has prompted a raging debate among feminists (see, for instance, Schor and Weed, 1994). Cultural Feminism, alternatively known as feminine feminism, essential feminism, domestic feminism, and difference feminism, among other descriptors, differs from more popular liberal feminist theory, which regards essentializing itself as the source of women's subordination. Cultural feminist theory, on the contrary, names the devaluation of women's essential differences (whether biologically based or culturally constructed) as problematic and as the root of sexism. Cultural feminists believe that women have developed their different identities, and in particular their unique social orientation, in the context of the domestic sphere. This value system gives women "the basis for the articulation of a humane world view, one which can operate to change the destructive masculine ideologies that govern the public world" (Donovan, 1992, pp. 60–61). Liberal feminists deny fundamental gender differences between women and men, arguing that true equality will be achieved when gender difference is erased; they believe that women and men are more alike than different, and that the vast majority of gender differences are the result of different and inequitable opportunities. According to Josephine Donovan:

> If male-female difference is not in the genes, then the assumption is that it must be a matter of social environment; if this is the case, then the traits that we attribute to women and men must be seen as mutable. A change in socialization, or education, or social circumstance would produce different gender identities or no such identities at all. We would all be "persons" or androgynes. This is the liberal feminist position.
> (1992, p. 61)

Cultural feminists, on the other hand, embrace gender differences, whether these stem from innate qualities or cultural circumstances, and they advocate a social climate that celebrates rather than denigrates such differences. Evelyn Nakano Glenn has dubbed this controversy the "equality–difference knot" (1994, p. 22).

Cultural feminist theory continues to attract proponents. Those interested in the social construction of motherhood have dominated the field (see Rich, 1976; Dinnerstein, 1976; Ruddick, 1983; Rothman, 1984; and Treblicot, ed., 1983). Theorists, in combination with poets, psychoanalysts, novelists, and others have tried to detach motherhood from a pronatalist ideology that ghettoizes the institution of motherhood; in its place they advance an ideology that posits a universal female experience of nurturing. A constellation of theories (often referred to collectively as "mothering theory") claims that the wisdom gained from the practice of motherhood can be used to understand gender and construct social theories rooted in "female values" like altruism and care.

As Judith Grant (1993) argues, mothering theorists have reversed the "personal is political" formulation by advocating a politics based on gendered values. Carol Gilligan's (1982) revision of psychological theories of gender and morality is typical of mothering theory's celebration of difference, which positions women's ways of seeing, feeling, and doing as distinct from men's and as a viable solution to many profound societal ills; see also Sara Ruddick's (1983) argument for "maternal thinking" as a theory of justice and world peace. Yet mothering theory has met with substantial criticism: "Exalting women's capacity to mother has contradictory implications for efforts to end women's subordination," Linda Blum and Elizabeth Vandewater charge, "as some use a woman-centered perspective to empower women while others use biological essentialism to constrain women's opportunities" (1993, p. 297).

Grant links difference theories to the pronatalist milieu of our times and characterizes the acceptance of mothering theory as a reaction to the religious Right's call for a return to fundamental family values—or, as she puts it, "an example of feminism on the run from the Right in the 1980s" (1993, p. 67). The mothering theorists' conception of women's experience is blind to the reality that "one's immediate perception of one's own experience is inevitably affected and skewed by the hegemonic culture (patriarchy, capitalism or both)," Grant argues (p. 59). Experiences of nurturing, caring, healing, and so on are hardly liberatory, since they occur in the context of patriarchy.

Mothering theory is a vital part of feminist discourse and forms the theoretical basis of natural mothering. But what does feminism have to do with a group of women who choose a lifestyle characterized by a traditionally gendered division of labor?

Nearly 50 percent of the women I studied identified as feminists to some degree (and they offered this political orientation without my prompting). Nearly all the remaining women expressed ideas compatible with feminist politics, but did not label themselves as such.[5] Only three of the 32 women interviewed expressed decidedly antifeminist views (and two of these women grounded their disagreement in their Christian conservatism). Many of the natural mothers encountered feminist ideology during their college years; some were active in movements defending choice, opposing violence against women, and promoting women's peace activism. What is especially consistent among them, however, is the type or form of feminism to which they subscribe. Cultural Feminism, as described in some detail above, is the feminism of natural mothering.

Certainly, Cultural Feminism is an influence on natural mothering, but communitarianism, environmentalism, and even Marxist socialism, for example, also shape both the practice and the ideology of natural mothering to differing degrees. Yet the natural mothers referred to this particular strain of feminist thought more than to any other coherent ideology. Their identity as feminists who celebrated their uniqueness as woman had a profound influence on their lifestyle choices. A feminism that not only recognizes but valorizes women's capacity to nurture *as* mothers forms a foundation to natural mothering. The women I interviewed expressed frustration with liberal feminism, which they perceived as "trying to get women to be just like men." Cultural Feminism, however, serves as an ideological link between their lifestyle as natural mothers and their commitment to women's equality. That is, they ground their daily lives in their identity as women uniquely equipped to nurture and take care of others. They assert the "fact" of their difference from men as the source of their strength. They are not interested in erasing or collapsing gender difference; they revel in it. And they revel in it precisely by practicing a style of mothering that foregrounds their identity as women. Furthermore, they express impatience with those they believe adopt a male standard and use it to measure's women's worth.

Although there is striking agreement about the version of feminism they espouse, not all the natural mothers use the terminology of Cultural Feminism. For instance, a few women spoke of their disapproval of "where the women's movement is going" or felt that the women's movement hurt mothers like them. They offered their own alternative vision of a feminism that not only supported but actually congratulated women for devoting themselves to raising the next generation of well-adjusted, gentle, loved, and peaceful children as a form of social change. When I told them that some of their views were compatible with a variant of feminist theory known generally as Cultural Feminism and elaborated its features, one exclaimed, "Wow! That's it!

That's what I have been saying!" (followed by apologies for "not reading more" and "being out of touch with stuff").

So, indeed, Cultural Feminism and more specifically mothering theory figure prominently in the construction of natural mothering, as do the Voluntary Simplicity and Attachment Parenting movements. The three intersect to form a unique lifestyle practice. From VS, natural mothering draws its commitment to "less is more," deriving meaning from austerity and anticonsumerism. From AP, it draws its rationale for uninterrupted mother–baby togetherness and, as from VS, an approach to parenting that places "people before things," as La Leche League proponents often say. Cultural Feminism injects a political element into the practice of natural mothering. Natural mothers, so many of them self-described feminists, maintain that their gender-specific lifestyle does not oppress them because it is grounded in a theory of women's differences from men as a source of power, not inequity, and therefore something to be celebrated and defended.

45. The Author's Argument: At the start of the 21st century, female moral Reform continues under a new guise. Todays maternalists embrace a notion That an essential female NATURE shapes The practices of motherhood and a larger female reality. Says There ARE essential differences between men & women.

47. Todays maternalists do not challenge The structure and content of gender relations

62. What happens when the real mothers & fathers make sacrifices necessary To reject aids such as bottles, pacifiers, strollers, and cribs? What happens when The mother must go to work outside The home? What does it cost to enact A lifestyle in which the child is The center of the universe? what kind of child produce?

64-65. The marketing hype of natural parenting/ attachment parenting.
67. cultural feminism & (68) names The devaluation of women's essential differences as problematic and The root of sexism
68. Liberal Feminism: Deny fundamental gender differences between men & women. (Says social difference is not in the genes). (seems extreme) To me

4 Interrogating the Ideology of Natural Mothering

Choice, Nature, and Inevitability

The Feminism in Natural Mothering

Because many of the natural mothers identified themselves as feminists or at the very least identified with feminist ideas, I wondered how they reconciled their feminist politics with a traditionally gendered lifestyle in which the father works outside the home, providing financial resources, and the mother works in and around it, providing unpaid care for family and home. I invited my informants to share their understandings of feminism. As we have seen, most women pledged allegiance to the broad aims of the movement, and in particular the pursuit of equal rights for women. Pay equity and equal opportunity were most commonly offered as important and worthy aims of the feminist agenda to which they subscribed. Some women were intimately involved in the women's movement; others were merely supportive.

Angela Cronon, mother of an 11-year-old son named Brooke, found great meaning in the feminist movement during the early years of the second wave. Angela, who holds a Ph.D. in ornithology and splits her time between a part-time position as a research scientist and homeschooling her preteen son, spoke emotionally about the role of feminist consciousness-raising groups in the 1970s in transforming her life and restoring her self-esteem.

> The women's movement had a strong impact on me, and I was a young adult woman at the time when consciousness-raising groups and that kind of thing first started. And I got involved in that, and I think one of the most powerful things was to begin to see that the conditions in your life and which you were experiencing weren't unique to you. And then to begin to look at why that was true. So that was very important to me.

Pat Lincoln, a retired environmental community organizer and full-time unschooling mother of two young boys, described her introduction to the movement:

> I first came across feminism in the tenth grade when a girl asked me, "Are you a male supremacist?" And I said, "I dunno. What is that?" And she said, "Do you believe the man should be the head of the household and make all the decisions?" And I said yes! (laughter). But within a year feminism caught up with me and that was all turned around. And I was incredulous that I ever thought that . . . I still am.

Still, each mother seemed to have exhausted the movement's relevance to her own life (as represented by the liberal feminist agenda of achieving equal status on men's terms) as she began the journey of motherhood. Kim Monroe, who attended a series of alternative schools and now unschools her two children in a rural area, admitted suppressing her "longing for family" as a young college student at a small, private, nontraditional college because such ideas were incompatible with women's movement ideology:[1]

"When I was an undergraduate, a woman wouldn't be caught dead admitting that family was one of her highest priorities. Still, I knew I had always longed for family."

Pat explained the shift from liberal feminist consciousness and its emphasis on achieving equity based on a "male standard" to a contrasting cultural feminist emphasis on women's biology and "natural" or "essential" tendencies as a source of women's power. She distanced herself from Western feminist ideology by criticizing its ignorance of the biological "roots" that shape gender identity and human relations: "Feminism arose out of a Western culture that is totally divorced of beliefs to [*sic*] what is our roots. It's not surprising, then, that Western feminists have a hard time with a lifestyle like mine."

Some women harbored a hostility toward the women's movement even while embracing its larger aims, such as social and economic equality for women. Interestingly, the three informants who espoused decidedly antifeminist sentiments took issue with the movement for what they regarded as its antimotherhood stance. But even the more moderate women and the large number who maintained a feminist identity took a dim view of the movement's treatment of motherhood; many felt personally offended by what they construed as a feminist rhetoric unsympathetic to mothers. Grace Burton, considered a natural mothering pioneer by some, describes herself as a "radical feminist," yet expresses a sense of betrayal and disenchantment with the women's movement:

> I feel that the women's movement of the sixties robbed me of something. It did get me more pay in the workplace, and I don't mind that, but they also made me *be* in the workplace, and I mind that immensely. The issues that I feel are strong feminist issues are birthing issues, medical issues, home issues, food

issues, and these aren't issues that have been addressed at all. The issue that's been addressed is, "Am I an equal person in society?" And I would like to be considered an equal person in society. But that doesn't mean I have to do the exact same things that somebody else does. I am not the same other person. I feel that someone, and I feel that it should be the woman, needs to be the focus of the family, to keep the family running, organized, on track, spiritually, physically, and emotionally.

As Grace said this, her voice began to tremble. When she finished, she looked at me and said, "I am sorry, but that's what I think." Her apology acknowledged that her sentiments may appear "out of step" with a more conventional feminist agenda (if one exists). Indeed, she may have feared that her disclosure was an act of feminist heresy.

I Am Not My Mother: The Centrality of Choice in Natural Mothering

Grace's "heresy" was not uncommon. In fact, the interviews revealed that most women were engaged in the same struggle to negotiate the rocky terrain between politics and life. They were aware of the complicated triangular relationship between a popular feminist agenda they once embraced, their current alternative lifestyle, and their changing view of what it means to be feminist. Ingrid Kitzinger, a former Peace Corps volunteer and mother of four children, interrupted my description of the research I was doing by exclaiming, "Feminists are horrified with me!" Michelle Jones-Grant, who earned a bachelor of arts in women's studies and English before beginning her family (today she regards that degree as "too esoteric"), addressed the ostensible contradiction between her politics and lifestyle.

She might not "look like much of a feminist"—"trooping around with my three kids, with no goal really before me

beyond getting through the early years with my children."
Yet she maintained that because she *chose* her lifestyle
actively and consciously, it was entirely consistent with a
feminist perspective—with Cultural Feminism, which celebrates the gendered distinctiveness of women, and in particular their unique ability to carry, give birth to, and care for
a child. The contradiction, she implied, is only superficial,
easily resolved for a feminist who acknowledges the essential experience of being a woman. She said:

> Choice. I've made lots of decisions to get where I am, and I
> think that probably differs [*sic*] me from somebody who . . . my
> neighbor over here was telling me [that] 30 years ago she
> moved in next door with children the same age as my chil-
> dren. She was at home with her kids because that's what was
> expected of her. It was clear that it wasn't ever a choice that
> she made. And I think that's a big defining thing.

But I still wondered how women *felt* about this division
of roles. Would their feminist consciousness indict the comfort they felt living a traditional lifestyle? Remembering
Betty Friedan's (1963) wrenching descriptions of full-time
mothers who overwhelmingly experienced ennui, alien-
ation, and hopelessness, I probed Kim to see if she felt
trapped. She assured me that she did not, and she empha-
sized the importance of choice in fashioning what appears a
"backward" lifestyle to some. In her characteristically meas-
ured style, she paused thoughtfully and replied: "Well, I
think it only can be a trap in so far as that's your perception.
If it's a choice, it can't be a trap, because if it's something you
feel strongly about and wish to do a great deal, and has
tremendous meaning to you, it's not a trap at all. It's self-
actualizing. It's living out goals, et cetera."

Chris Johnson-Fairchild once worked outside the home
while her husband stayed home full-time with their young

children. She currently works one night shift per week as a social worker at a human service agency. Chris echoed Michelle's and Kim's sentiments. She too recognized that the appearance and the reality of natural mothering may be at odds. In other words, natural mothering may seem a life of self-sacrifice and subordinated personal needs that no thinking woman would choose, least of all a self-described feminist, but such an assessment fails to see below the surface. Like other mothers, Chris invoked a historical comparison to highlight the importance of choice. When I asked how she reconciled her feminist politics with her traditional lifestyle, Chris mused that the natural mothering variant of the stay-at-home mother might *appear* retrograde, but there are fundamental differences. One of the most important is the woman's actively choosing this lifestyle with eyes wide open, cognizant of both costs and benefits:

> It's a new thing. It's not going back. Jim and I joke, but sometimes he comes [in] and he says, "June! June! I'm home." And the kids run down, "Daddy, Daddy, Daddy." It's like, here we are in a 1960s house, living this traditional thing. Okay, so this is what they're growing, sort of what I grew up with, but they don't have a TV, which puts it in a certain . . . This is our best hope, is that it's going to come out different. Some of the factors look the same on the outside, but because there are different feelings inside, this is a choice, and they know that Mom does go to work and has worked, and they remember, because we talk about "when Dad was home, when you [Mom] weren't home with us," they have a memory of that, a memory that we keep alive, and that it will come out this whole different way.

Like Michelle, Kim, and others, Chris emphasizes choice. This is crucial to understanding how natural mothers make sense of their lives. Before they became mothers, many of the women easily supported a liberal agenda focused on succeeding on men's terms in contemporary society. But something caused them to reconsider what it meant to be a feminist in the late twentieth century, and that something was motherhood. But even as mother-feminists, the natural mothers did not wholly reject their "old feminism." Although they rejected their former belief that women, in order to achieve social equality, must gain access to the sources of power men have historically kept off limits to them, they continued to embrace the notion that "feminism is about women having the right to make choices," as one put it. This feminist legacy of "choice as a right" figured prominently as they adapted their "new feminism" to their current lifestyle as natural mothers.

And *choice,* according to the natural mothers, is the key distinction between them and mothers of previous eras or different social contexts who also stayed or stay home devoting their full energies to childrearing and homemaking.[3] Because these women, usually in partnership with their husbands, have weighed their options and elected to lead a deliberately traditional lifestyle, their lives are indeed consistent with a broad feminist ideology, they reason. That is, they told me, as long as women are not coerced to live out a particular set of actions, whatever those actions may be (and whatever others may think of those actions), charges of antifeminism or oppression are ill-fitting. The natural mothers claim that any critic need only look beneath the surface of their lives to their intelligent and conscious choice making to see that they are unlike (middle-class) women who had or have no choice but to devote themselves to the service of husband, children, and home.

Nevertheless, when I probed for the precise reasons for their choice, a complicated picture emerged. It became clear to me that their claims of personal agency were exaggerated.

The boundary between choice and trap, so sharp and solid to the natural mothers, looks fuzzy to me.[4] Before I describe the limits on personal choice making that I discovered, I will note the constraints the natural mothers claim they do *not* experience.

The women I interviewed were certain that *no one* had overtly forced them to practice full-time, intensive, natural homemaking and childrearing. This was not what I originally anticipated. When I first approached this topic, I expected to hear tales of oppressive husbands demanding that their wives live out the goals of Voluntary Simplicity and Attachment Parenting, much like the men of Fruitlands, who theorized the communal lifestyle and left its enactment to the women (see Chapter 3). Or I anticipated stories about husbands who paid lip-service to mothers' rights to balance career and paid work but made such a balancing act impossible. Were the natural mothers partnered with men who refused to pick up a broom or spatula, thereby forcing the wives to abandon careers outside the home because it was just too hard to work what Arlie Hochschild (1989) terms "the second shift"?

I heard no such tales. Instead, several women stated that they were at cross-purposes with mates who would prefer their wives to work outside the home and bring in additional income or enrich their partnership. For instance, Bob Dittmer encouraged his wife, Carrie, to return to her work in state-funded childcare and parent-education management. He believed that Carrie's working for pay would not only raise the family's standard of living but foster a more collegial relationship between them. He wanted to broaden and deepen their conversations with mutual "shop talk" (since he too worked in the social service field), while making it possible to acquire, in Carrie's words, "nice things."

But Carrie did not share Bob's thirst for a change in their lifestyle. She was much more willing to "go without and make do."

Just prior to our interview, Bob expressed interest in buying a home computer, whereas Carrie saw such a purchase as unnecessary; they already had a functioning word processor that met her basic needs: "It's still faster than writing a letter by hand." Similarly, Mary Schwartz's first husband consistently resisted her commitment to parent full-time and simplify their life. Mary, who has been one algebra course away from earning her bachelor's degree for several years, explained that her former husband's need for "nice things" was out of step with her need for a healthy, family-centered lifestyle. Eventually this value clash led to their divorce. Mary is now happily married to George, who works a reduced workweek so that he can spend more time at home with their new baby and Mary's son from her first marriage. According to Mary, he is not concerned with updating their household appliances, driving a nice car, or wearing fashionable clothes. She considers herself "very lucky to have found a man like George." So if male coercion is not at the root of the natural mother's choice to live an alternative, simplified, family-centered lifestyle, what is?

Again and again, the natural mothers I spoke with assured me that the only reason they chose the life they lead was a personal compulsion to do what they considered "best for my family." Instead of stories of frustrated career goals and unhelpful husbands, I heard an imaginative inventory of what life would be like if the mothers attempted to combine career and family. (In a few cases the description was based on experience.) They rejected the rushed and harried existence they were sure such a dual life entailed. They envisioned a way of life that held absolutely no appeal for them. They chose to mother full-time because they feared an unmanageable alternative. "To get ahead in the workplace in many fields, you still have to pretty much be a neglectful mother," Carrie mused. She remembered, with a shudder, the struggle she endured when she combined mothering a young baby and taking college courses. For her, it was simply too stressful:

> I feel like when they are young I can't imagine working any more than I have, when they're young. It's been hard enough . . . It's been hard enough the times I've tried to take classes. I didn't do that with him (points to her second-born, a four-year-old boy), because it was too stressful for me when my daughter was this age. We had more tantrums and things, because I think the kids this age have an inherent need to not be very regulated, to kind of go with the flow more, and that when you're on a tight schedule yourself, you force your kids to be on a tight schedule.

For Carrie, when Mom works outside the home, kids suffer. She doesn't ask how fathers and others might mediate this process by pitching in and shouldering childcare. Although she attributes her decision to stay out of the paid labor force to the children's best interests, it is not difficult to see how her lifestyle was shaped by the structural constraints of a family-unfriendly college (with inconveniently timed classes, for example) and a husband unable or unwilling to alter his "tight schedule" to better accommodate family needs (and avert "more tantrums and things").

Jenny Strauss's sentiments echoed Carrie's. Previously a successful and well-paid physical therapist and now the mother of three boys ranging in age from six to 14, Jenny expressed "absolutely no interest" in returning to the workforce even now that all three of her children are of school age and gone from the home five to six hours a day:

JS: To me it was, I can't be a great mom and do that [work outside the home] . . . or maybe a realistic assessment of really what your time and energy is. I mean, I couldn't go out and be a full-time PT and do what I do.

CB: Even if you did it while the kids were at school?

JS: No, I couldn't. Because you can't do it while the kids are at school. Well, you can, but then you can't do any of the things you do now when the kids are at school. So what does that mean? That means that I'd have to take one evening a week and go grocery shopping, which sounds like [a] small undertaking, except that the way our lives are in the evening, that is a major undertaking. To try and find that. And if I didn't do it then, I'd do it on the weekend and it would take twice as long, because it's crowded.

sounds like — complacation

Jenny's story reveals more than a distaste for crowded grocery stores. Certainly it reflects her honest assessment of the constraints on her time imposed by outside factors such as children's evening activities, the press of crowds that slow errands, and the endless list of "things to do" uniquely assigned to Mom. Her inventory of what needs to be done on a daily basis leaves no room for work outside the home, given the structure of her family's time. It appears to be incumbent upon Jenny to accommodate her children's and her husband's varied and demanding schedules and somehow fit the rest of her obligations into the gaps that remain. To her, pulling that off is what constitutes being a "great mom." How could she possibly achieve this tenuous balancing act with the added stress of a constant daytime commitment?

Unlike Carrie, who appeals to children's inherent needs, Jenny is fully aware of the structural constraints that shape her decision to remain primary caregiver and mother-manager for her family. Her decision to detach from the workforce is strategically inspired to avoid stress—perhaps the only source of stress she is able to control. And so she does. By limiting the additional stressors in her life, she feels that she clears her way to be a better, more efficient mother to her family.

To help me understand why they had fashioned an alternative lifestyle, some mothers invoked the figure I eventually termed the "bad other mother." This mother—the antithesis of the natural mother—makes few conscious choices. Rather, she "goes with the flow" of the mainstream, seldom questioning the conventional wisdom that dictates so much of parenting practice. This mother is neither evil nor malicious, the natural mothers tell me; she is simply ignorant—duped by a powerful, child-hostile, expert- and institution-dependent culture. The "bad other mother" has her babies by planned cesarean section. She bottle-feeds because she does not want to be bothered by breastfeeding. She feeds her children hotdogs and potato chips for lunch because it is quick and easy. When her children complain of an ear infection, she demands antibiotics but cannot understand why her children are chronically ill. She uses the television as an electronic babysitter. But perhaps the most common characterization of the "bad other mother" is the woman who insists that she must work, but really does so only "to support her addiction to materialism and careerism," as one mother said.

Kim, who rejected the view of the natural mother as trapped by traditionalism, related the story of her twin sister, who has chosen to pursue a demanding career while raising two small children. In defense of her own decision to structure her life around her children, Kim portrayed her sister as the classic working mother—overextended, gravely unhappy, and "sacrificing her children." To Kim, it is her sister who is trapped by her own materialism and ill-fated quest for success, all because she has put her own needs before her children's:

> KM: I have a twin sister . . . she's well-known and all that. She's a miserable person. She's extremely busy. She has to hire nannies to take care of her own children, which I think really grieves her. Feels trapped by all the responsibilities, and yet is so seduced, I think, or least in the beginning was so seduced, by the idea of being a success in the classic sense, of making a lot of money and being kind of a well-known figure in a certain community, that she can't step away from it. And at the same time, she is aware, now that she has two children, that they're being sacrificed, their needs are being sacrificed. And I think it causes her a lot of anguish. I know it causes her a lot of anguish.
>
> CB: What does she think of your lifestyle?
>
> KM: I think she's envious. It's caused a lot of conflict in our relationship because I think that she admires me and envies me and feels very, very frustrated that she hasn't been able to make the kind of choices I have. She perceives me—she puts me up on a pedestal, that, too. I suppose she perceives . . . making choices in your children's . . . interest to be the greatest good, and she feels that I've at least certainly succeeded in doing that. Whereas she doesn't view that she—she, I think, somehow feels that she's failed, even though she tries very hard in her limited way to be involved in their lives.[5]

Career-minded mothers, warns Kim's cautionary tale, produce suffering children. In Kim's view, however, her sister's "problem" can be corrected, because different *choices* are all that separates the two sisters. When Kim distances herself from her sister, led astray by "social measuring rods of success," her alternative life stands apart as one constructed by the careful and deliberate consideration of each parenting act. In fact, the bulk of "bad other mother" stories operate in much the same way.

Stories like Kim's were regularly invoked to prove the point that others choose wrongly. And their mistaken choices are evidenced by their harried, "miserable" lives. The natural mothers pride themselves on steering clear of the rushed life, the money- and status-driven life, ultimately, the unexamined life. The natural mothers tell me that they have risen above this fray and are never, ever going back. Yet while they criticize others for paying homage to socially constructed values that effectively discourage individuality, creativity, and a richer quality of life in general, they fail to acknowledge the ways in which their own ideas are socially constructed. It is others—others who question neither institutions like hospitals and schools nor authorities like physicians and teachers—who permit others to think for them.

The natural mothers profess to operate in a realm virtually untouched by social influence. Their ideas, supposedly rooted in nature and fostered by their waxing self-confidence, are not the products of culture, but the products of nature. Natural mothering, then, is an organic experience. The experience of natural mothering is available to any woman who sheds her trust of others and taps into her trust in nature, a trust realized when she begins to trust herself. The natural mothers hope (and, yes, *trust*) that others will follow their lead. Yet their notion of freely made choice is thrown into question by their own perception of *thinking* as subordinate to *feeling*.

A Mother's Embodied Knowledge

When I asked women to explain why they constructed a child-centered, mother-dependent, simplified lifestyle, I heard a similar refrain: natural mothering respects and reflects our nature as females. Women are designed, with wombs, breasts, and "the mothering hormone" (oxytocin) to nurture children.[6] Men are not. A father's role is no less important to the care and development of children, but it is clearly different and, at least in the child's earliest years, requires less intimate contact. Grace Burton, who had earlier apologized for her unconventional, ostensibly "antifeminist" views, offered the following impassioned explanation:

> The traditional roles are in place because men are physically stronger and, therefore, would be the people who would go out and be the hunters and . . . the people who built the structures that one lives in, and those kinds of things. Whereas Mother Nature has given woman the position of bringing the next generation to fruition in her own body and, in addition to that, has provided her body with the ability to nourish and nurture that infant, at least until the age of one—literally nourish until the age of one. I believe that. I did it. So, then, why should it be wrong for the woman to continue that role?

✓ oversimplified

Roles flow from bodies in this view. According to the natural mothers, humans are predestined to act out certain roles as dictated by the structure and function of biological bodily processes.[7]

The natural mothers I spoke with arrived at this understanding in a variety of ways. Some, like Grace, had "always" held a gendered set of beliefs relative to childrearing and domesticity. A greater number of women came to believe in a biological basis for the gendered division of labor once they read a particular book, for instance, that inspired them to regard biology as primary. Several mentioned the eye-opening experience of reading Jean Liedloff's *The Continuum Concept* (1985), which "spoke to their hearts" and reinforced what they felt intuitively. The book, now in its nineteenth printing, has a significant international following. Liedloff practices and teaches psychotherapy based on *The Continuum Concept* and lectures and broadcasts internationally. The Liedloff Continuum Network maintains a website and in late 1997 initiated a discussion listserv that draws subscribers from South Africa, the Netherlands, Great Britain, Australia, New Zealand, Germany, and the United States. Pat Lincoln's recollection of her first encounter with the book is representative.

> The book *The Continuum Concept* is another mind-altering experience. Babies have expectations, and the most important expectation is to be with mother all the time until it starts to crawl. The fact that expectations are routinely violated is the root of a lot of troubles in the world. Once you know that, all these ideologies [feminist thought] don't matter much any more. They are interesting and true in many ways, *but they are trying to deny who we are.* [Emphasis mine.]

Others sought out La Leche League for breastfeeding support and discovered, to their delight, that "League" (as it is called) was a font of mothering guidance that extended far beyond the how-tos of breastfeeding. Theresa Reyes described the almost spiritual quality of attending monthly meetings: "Going there month after month, I felt like I was going to church. I would come away feeling the importance of being a mother." Most importantly, League unearthed and reinforced beliefs that the women discovered they had always "known" but couldn't express. Kim Monroe's words capture this nicely: "La Leche League philosophy only [sic] again really reinforced convictions I had that *came from the heart* about what I felt was the appropriate thing for me to do for my children" (emphasis mine).

La Leche League's most celebrated publication, *The Womanly Art of Breastfeeding* (1958), had a similarly life-transforming effect on several of the mothers I interviewed. For a number of women, reading the book was "like a bible experience" as one mother put it. Michelle Jones-Grant read it "cover to cover" in the hospital and was amazed at how the authors articulated precisely what she felt but had not been able to express. This notion of ideas coming from the heart, of "just knowing" something to be true but lacking the ability to express it, pervaded natural mothering discourse. Over and over again, women described the sensation of "knowing deep inside" or understanding something that defied description but was nonetheless strongly felt. For example, when I asked Carrie Dittmer how she arrived at her decision to parent in an unconventional way, she appeared mystified at first but eventually replied: "I had certain ideas back in high school, back in the early 1970s, of when I became a parent what I would do. And they just seemed like the ways that made the most sense. . . . It never crossed my mind to do anything other than to breastfeed and to nurse as long as my kids wanted to . . . until they stopped."

If practices or ideas must "make sense" to be viable, how does a woman know what is sensible? For most of the natural mothers, if something seemed or felt "natural," that was good enough. One mother answered my query, "Why did you decide to have a family bed?" with: "You know, the idea of the family bed just seemed so *natural.*"

I probed further. How do you know something makes sense? What is natural and what is not? What is your criterion for distinguishing "right" parenting practices from "wrong" ones? I encountered puzzled, searching stares and long silences. It was clear that "just knowing" defied further description. My questions missed the point as far as they were concerned. If something felt right, that meant that it transcended the intellectual realm. It could not be explained or reasoned. "Just knowing" was an intuitive sensation, not one that could be intelligently and precisely explained with words. It was something felt deep inside. Take, for instance, Denise Grant, mother of four Waldorf-educated children,[8] wife of a physician, and recent "graduate" of a direct-entry midwifery apprenticeship,[9] who wondered aloud how she would know if natural mothering fulfilled its promise of producing happier, better-adjusted children, as compared with more mainstream childrearing:

> And how would you ever know, when you see kids from families like this and they're 30 and you go interview them. Is it because their parents were educated, world travelers, or is it because of the parenting method? How are you ever gonna really know? *But I just know in my heart.* That's all I can do, is just say: in my heart I think I'm making a big difference in the world through my kids. *But it can't be proven scientifically.* [Emphasis mine.]

Denise relied on her personal convictions while recognizing that it is nearly impossible to establish a true cause-and-effect relationship in this case. When I probed further, she tried to identify the reasons for her approach to parenting, but the best she could do was repeat that she "just knew deep in [her] heart that it was right." Then she offered the following story. When Denise's son Sam was three and a half years old, the two of them regularly attended a weekly YMCA parent–tot swim class. Sam enjoyed the one-on-one time with his mom, but as soon as the swim instructor called the parents and kids into a large group circle, little Sam would start screaming. "It was way too overwhelming," Denise reasoned. To calm Sam, Denise would excuse herself and the child from the circle and retreat to a corner to nurse him discreetly. She wondered if anybody noticed but refused to allow others' opinions to sway her because, in her words, "I just knew. I just had total conviction." Intrigued by Denise's unwavering confidence, I asked, "*How* did you know?"

I don't know. It was just there. I just never wavered. This is the
way that was right for us, period. I never had any doubt. . . .
You just have to keep going back to: How can you spoil them
by keeping them close and loving them? They're only babies.
Three and a half is a baby. It is not an independent citizen in
the society. It's a baby. They're just taking more time to unfold
than some other kids.

It is clear that the reasons for natural mothering are often
literally beyond reason. Rather than being rooted in an epistemology derived from the intellect, this type of "knowing"
is intuitive, even instinctual and therefore defies explanation, the natural mothers imply. Decisions are not ultimately
based on thinking, but on feeling. Choosing a family bed,
child-led weaning, or home birth is not based on reading a
good book or even hearing a compelling argument,
although those experiences often _name_ dearly held beliefs
that inform these decisions. Indeed, many natural mothers
rely on the role models and the information in books to
assist them in making decisions. But in the final analysis, a
particular practice must _feel_ right (and not a single woman
in this study said that natural mothering did _not_ feel right).
The expression "from the heart" reifies the body-centered
consciousness central to this epistemology.[10] Again, instruc-
tions on the proper way to mother are located within one's
own body and known by the triggering of certain feelings.
For natural mothers, feeling both prefigures and constitutes
her alternativity.

Despite the shared reliance on "just knowing," each of
the natural mothers experienced this epistemological shift at
a different time in her mothering career, suggesting yet
again that "natural living" does not necessarily come naturally. The issue of returning to work after the birth of the
first child is illustrative. A small number of women were

clear before they became mothers that intensive, child-centered mothering was their choice, but nearly half of the women I interviewed had planned to return to work shortly after the birth of their first child, only to discover, once the baby arrived, as one woman declared emphatically: "There was no way I was gonna leave this child!"

After hearing a large number of similar stories describing changed plans and transitions to stay-at-home motherhood, I eventually labeled such revelatory narratives "shock-shift stories." These stories unfolded predictably. Soon after the birth of her first child, the new mother was *shocked* by her overwhelming feelings of love for her baby and her companion feelings of being unable to leave him or her. Next, she *shifted* her perspective from that of a pregnant woman with careerist aspirations to that of a new mother who simply had to be with her baby around the clock. For her, there was no alternative, no choice. Theresa described her conversion:

> TR: I figured I would continue working. . . . Then after I had the baby I changed my mind about going back to work. I just couldn't trust leaving, not being able to breastfeed the baby on demand, and I didn't want to leave the baby with my husband with a bottle, because I knew she would cry.
>
> CB: Were you surprised with your feelings?
>
> TR: *I just felt I had no choice,* and I thought I could do those things, well (sigh), I thought he could feed the baby formula while I was gone. I suppose I was a little surprised, because after she was born it was not an option for me to leave her, whereas before *it was maybe an option for me to leave her* with her dad while we worked opposite shifts. But I just wanted to take care of her myself full-time, and I wanted to breastfeed her full-time. [Emphasis mine.]

Theresa resolved her difficult situation by staying home. For her, a mother is instinctually the superior care-provider for a child. Others will not suffice. It is difficult to know what circumstances in Theresa's life might have led her to a different choice: A more confidence-inspiring husband? A calmer baby? A more compelling job outside the home?

Carrie Dittmer's "shock-shift" story offers a bit of insight into Theresa's dilemma by suggesting that a natural mother's intensity of feeling figured more prominently than the role of even the best-intentioned husband/father. Like Theresa, Carrie surprised herself with the intensity of her attachment to her new daughter. It made it difficult for her to share parenting responsibilities with her husband, in spite of his willingness to parent equally.

> I hadn't expected the intensity of feeling that I would have. So that once she was born there was no way I was going to let anyone else take care of her. And I was so hooked in with her that it was hard even for my husband, because his first two kids had been bottle-fed and so he had been able to be a much more equal partner in feeding them and things. So that was very hard for him—that she only wanted me. I tried pumping milk so that he could feed her, even though it was actually hard for me to think of her taking a bottle, but I would pump milk so that he could feed her and so that my stepkids could feed her, because they wanted to do that. And she wouldn't take a bottle. She was one of those kids who wouldn't take it at all. And so I couldn't leave her for even an hour or two with my husband to go do anything. . . . I was so attached to her, I don't think I shared her as much, and I felt I was partly responsible for the fact that I couldn't leave her with him; it wasn't that he wasn't willing.

From this passage, it is unclear whether Carrie's discomfort with having others provide care to her daughter ultimately sabotaged such efforts. One wonders to what extent her self-worth is derived from her children's dependency. Clearly, however, her intense feelings of attachment structured the division of childcare in spite of prebirth expectations (and the father's and stepchildren's wishes). Carrie was clearly unprepared for her feelings and the way they prevented others from being involved in the care of a new family member. For her as for the natural mothers in general, feelings that "came from the heart" established the patterns of family life, and these feelings always led to a biologically derived division of family labor. This theme recurred throughout the interviews.

Denise Grant, the midwife and the mother of four children, had originally planned to pursue her midwifery studies after the birth of her first child. But she chucked her plans to begin her apprenticeship once she experienced what for her was an undeniable attachment to her baby: "It wasn't until I held my first baby that I realized—I'm going to leave this baby in the middle of the night? To go take care of some lady? And I had—I knew in my heart it wasn't feeling right. I couldn't do that. . . . And so I had that huge realization, because I was planning on just becoming a midwife whenever I could."

Pat Lincoln intended to balance career and motherhood but, to her surprise, found that her attachment to her new baby prevented her from returning to the workforce:

> I had planned to return to my job after six months. After all, everybody I ever knew or ever heard of did that. But as the six months came up, I started having all these dreams. I am riding my bike to work, and I realize I have left the baby at home alone. I was pretty conflicted about going back to work. All the guys said you shouldn't promote a woman because she is just gonna leave when she has a baby, and I would always say, "Oh, that's not true." So I felt that if I didn't go back to work I was letting down feminism. But then I decided: What is more important? Your pride? Or what is best for your child?

This mother perceived a forced choice between supporting the feminist movement by proving her co-workers wrong and doing what was best for her child. This dualistic conceptualization wove throughout the interviews as women described facing a showdown between career and family. As they see it, mothers must ultimately choose between a demanding career and a good relationship with the family. No accommodations or compromises are possible. The only solution is to "follow their hearts" and choose "what feels right." And the assumption is that when a mother searches her heart and soul, what "feels right" is full-time, intensive, alternative mothering. This forced-choice paradigm directly contradicts the natural mothers' discourse of free choice. It raises the question: Did these women freely choose their life circumstances, or did their "hearts" choose for them?

Angela Cronon, who strongly identifies with feminism, provided yet another example of this feeling-based, body-derived epistemology. She and her husband had planned to divide the work of caring for their baby equally, but once the baby arrived, she was surprised to discover what for her was a biological reality. The following exchange is illustrative:

> AC: In our experience, there were times my bond with my daughter was a lot stronger than Bud's. A lot of our role-sharing plans just didn't work out. It was harder for my husband to make the accommodation to being a parent than I think it was for me.
>
> CB: Why was that?
>
> AC: I think that there are built-in biological realities.

And so it seems that the natural mothers further modified their feminist orientation to accommodate what they perceived as essential, biological differences between men and women. And this altered feminist perspective was initiated by sensations of "just knowing" something to be true.

The natural mothers' intellectual sense of the way things *should* be was quickly overridden by their experience of the way things really *were*. The body not only determines social practice, in this view; it literally sends messages in the form of "gut feelings" or "intuitive sensations." The body is a source of doing, knowing, and feeling. Interestingly, no one expressed regret or disillusionment at this "discovery." Instead, the mothers seemed to take this newfound understanding in stride, reworking the meaning that motherhood (and, correspondingly, fatherhood and paid careers) would have in their lives.

The relative ease with which the natural mothers adjusted to their "discoveries" leads to yet another set of questions. Is their subscription to a theory of biological destiny simply an after-the-fact rationalization for a lifestyle they had not imagined for themselves? Is the biology-as-destiny rationale a (perhaps unconscious) way of neutralizing ambivalence about a hyper-feminized existence that many of the women had rejected in earlier years? Take, for instance, Kim Monroe's interpretation of women's roles over the lifespan, roles predetermined and fixed by biology, as one way of justifying intensive motherhood:

> KM: I think women have different sets of stages in their lives than men. There is the mothering stage where your [*sic*] focus should be on her children and mothering, and I think that as a result of her commitment to her children she is more equipped to lead an incredibly productive life. I do think that motherhood has many more responsibilities than fatherhood. I see fathers as providing stability and emotional support to mothers and, most of all, financial support. The mother, by virtue of her role, can't be engaged in other spheres of interest.
>
> CB: Is that a biological fact?
>
> KM: (Pause) Yes. Because of the nursing.

Kim's conceptualization assumes that women must willingly submit to biology's shaping of their lives. Whatever the implications of this sort of body-dependent, feeling-based epistemology are, its centrality in natural mothering undermines the mother's claim of personal agency and free will as the impetus for her lifestyle. Natural mothering, it appears, is less a lifestyle fashioned by individual women making hard choices about the best way to parent than a chosen lifestyle represented in essentialist terms.

The paradox

The natural mothers who claim that they *chose* their lifestyle, acting as subjects or agents of their own destiny, simultaneously speak of the indisputable logic of nature that compels them to live out their lives. The mothers' passionate descriptions of "just knowing" and the kind of body-derived wisdom that once tapped into can never again be denied suggest a certain hegemony at work. These women are not forced by anyone (especially not husbands in any directly discernible way) to act as natural mothers, but personal agency is largely absent from their lives as natural mothers.

Some may counter that natural mothers surrender self-interest in the interest of their families but still maintain their personal agency. It certainly appears that way if we listen to only one-half of what the natural mothers are saying. If we listen to their narratives of self-motivated decisions to quit jobs and careers and stay at home full-time with babies, we see strong, self-determined women who actively choose a particular lifestyle, even if that lifestyle denies the individual mother's self-actualization. But if we listen a bit more closely, tuning into their motivations to mother in this particular way, a different picture comes into focus. Take, for example, Helen Rector's statement: "Once I realized there was this whole other way of being a parent [that] made such sense, I knew I could never go back."

I suspect that if Helen were challenged, she would likely acknowledge that she *could* "go back" if forced to, but it would be the kind of choice that feels inauthentic, a "Hobson's choice" (i.e., a choice between taking what is offered or nothing at all). Natural mothers like Helen may actively choose to embrace the "nature is best" ideology, but once they become attached to this ideology—buying into it completely and without regret—they surrender their capacity to make choices and in some ways become passive objects. Put differently, the ideology begins to take on hegemonic proportions and transforms women into individuals who surrender their own agency in the interest of family.

In *Social Movements in Advanced Capitalism,* Steven Buechler defines agency as "conscious, rational subjects acting collectively on their own interests" (2000, p. 177). Implied in this definition is a clear element of *thought:* An agent is one who *thinks* through a course of action, making active choices based on available information regarding how to act, who to be, and so on. The evidence presented in this chapter (and in the next) shows something quite different happening in the lives of the natural mothers. Rather than *thinking* through their options as parents, they draw their insight from feelings that cannot be explained or reasoned. The mothers speak of feeling the power of nature as they give birth, as they nurse, as they soothe their cranky children, and that power has irreversibly changed their lives.

But this raises an important question. Don't these women have a choice, in their view, to be bad mothers and shortchange their children? The answer is complicated. Theoretically speaking, the natural mothers claim that they *could* certainly choose to parent like "everyone else" (i.e., like the majority of conventional, mainstream mothers), but at the same time they speak of choice, they speak of being guided by an intuitive, body-derived source of knowledge, one that is undeniable, one that they can never dispute or reject. They sum up this knowledge simply: "Nature's way is the best way," and now that they *know* (read: *feel*) this, they cannot choose to parent any other way. It follows that there is, practically speaking, no *real* choice to parent differently. Natural mothering is the only real choice. The natural mothers in this study were adamant that they cannot turn their backs on the natural ideology so central to their way of living, sleeping, eating, schooling, and consuming. "Now that I've seen the light" (as one woman phrased it), conventional parenting is unfathomable.

It might be an overstatement to claim that the natural mothers have replaced God or Man as the authority that dictates a life course with nature as represented by the body, but perhaps not. Whether the mothers are controlled by men or religion or some conception of nature, they are still controlled. Again and again, the natural mothers told me that they "just knew" that natural mothering was right; they could not mother in any other way and live with themselves. The choice to embrace the ideology of "nature is best" was, in a sense, the last choice they made. All subsequent choices (what to buy, how to treat an illness, how to prepare food) flow from this ideology. I argue that constructing a lifestyle on the basis of a body-derived feeling that can neither be explained nor denied is the action not of an agent, but of an individual who is dutifully following a script. In this case the script was written by biologically determinist and historically gendered ideas about women, mothers, and families.

BoBel: logic Based

While Theresa Reyes gazed at the rows of paintings depicting the closeness of mothers and babies, she knew she longed for the same intimate bond with her own children some day. Years later, married and the mother of four, she reports that she got just that. Through extended breast-feeding and a host of other alternative practices, Theresa forged a connection with her children that she hails as unparalleled. And she says that she chose natural mother-ing fully aware of the costs. She was ready to "give herself over" to her children—"all the selfishness was all out" of her. To capture that mother–child bond she so desired, Theresa abandoned a promising career as a research scientist for full-time, natural motherhood.

Theresa's is the story of a woman disenchanted with the fast-paced, competitive life of hard science and professional-ism. It is also the tale of a woman faced with the burden of single-handedly managing a household and four children. She could have finished her graduate studies and pursued a challenging career in virology, but she opted for something else, something she regards as altogether better. For her, the choice to mother full-time, devoting her full energies to home and hearth, was not a "sellout" or a "copout." Rather, it was a choice to be sensible and down to earth.

A deeper analysis of Theresa's narrative reveals a more complicated tale of decision making mediated by an ideology of the body and the reality of gender relations. Theresa admits that she felt that she "had no choice" but to stay at home with her babies. Plans for her husband to bottle-feed "proved" unsatisfactory; nor could she tolerate even the possibility that her babies would struggle with their separa-tion from her. One picture—the educated scientist electing to mother in a certain way based on the best available infor-mation—gives way to another, the new mother who bases her decisions on sensation.

Furthermore, given Theresa's disenchantment with the labor force (and low labor-force attachment), leaving her nascent career behind likely caused her little anguish. The standards and norms established in her field were unappealing. Motherhood presented itself as an attractive alternative. Still, when I queried Theresa on her reasons for adopting specific practices, she invoked a rhetoric of social change. For example, she justified her commitment to extended breastfeeding by citing a voluminous body of data demonstrating the superiority of long-term nursing for the baby's and mother's health and the potential for breastfeeding to "make an incredible difference in the world." Theresa believes passionately that the breastfed child is better-adjusted and, accordingly, better equipped to cope with the challenges of everyday living. Breastfeeding may well save the world, in her view. But scratch the surface of this mother-activist's account and a woman living out her biological destiny is revealed.

Theresa's story represents a key thematic tension: between a life constructed freely and a life determined by the body. The natural mothers argue, some vehemently, that they *chose* a lifestyle that harks back to older, more rigidly defined gender roles, a time when women provided unpaid labor to family and home while men worked for pay in the public sphere. (This history, I would note, is bounded by class and race and is, moreover, in many ways illusory).[11] In fact, the natural mothers' so-called choice is less an enactment of free will and more a gendered acceptance of an ideology of biology as destiny.

When I asked individual women what separated them from women of earlier generations who also homeschooled, gave birth at home, engaged in extended nursing, and so on, I heard the strikingly familiar refrain of *choice*. "There are different feelings behind my life," one mother said. A paraphrase of the natural mothers' discourse might sound something like this: "I am not my mother. I chose this. I don't have to do it. I can always go back to work. I don't have to homeschool. I can accept an anesthetized birth. I can shop at the corporate grocery store. But I don't because I have evaluated the costs and benefits associated with each of those paths, and my values lie with the alternative life. I am living my life consciously and critically. I choose to swim outside the mainstream because it is in my family's best interest to do so."

Yet this narrative of choice is significantly undermined by the natural mothers' own stories of "just knowing" something to be true, of something making sense (without being able to explain why). The same women who invoked free choice regaled me with emotional tales of the profound wisdom found when a mother turns to her body's logic and intuition. The shock-shift stories, such as Pat Lincoln's remembrance of a dream that sent her a clear and undeniable message that home with baby was the only place to be, suggest that natural mothers made few choices but rather surrendered to what appeared obvious and ultimately inevitable—the belief that a mother is designed (by nature) to be home with her baby. In this conceptualization, anything else is a betrayal of our bodies and our families. Yet if the body dictates a proper course of action, women are not making an active and unconstrained choice about what to do. The essentialized decision is a surrender to the body, to an ideology of woman as caregiver. The natural mothering rationale accommodates patriarchal visions of women and mothers by reifying women as primary caregivers destined, because their lives are dictated by nature, to act in a limited capacity.

What ultimately differentiates my informants from earlier full-time, stay-at-home mothers is ideology. Today's natural mother invokes a rhetoric of choice, while women of earlier periods who embraced a domestic ideology would have invoked a rhetoric of obligation. Beneath the rhetoric in both cases, however, is the enactment of body-based, gender-role-bound behavior; the mothers regard their bodies as sources of knowledge. The natural mother's choice, then, is to situate her choice in an asocial conceptualization of the body in the interest of serving her children. While the mothers could choose to ignore this body-based knowledge, doing so would, in their view, imperil their children. And this is not a choice they can make. Their conception of free choice shaped only by personal preference and circumstance is illusory.

75. some of the natural mothers are awake of their political stance and the contradictions of "natural mothering".

75- NM: "says western feminist ideology is cut off from our (women's) roots."

75 NM: "the feminist movement made me be in the workplace"

76-77 NM: choice: a key distinction, according to the natural mothers

80. NM: said no one has ~~at~~ made them or forced them to practice ~~AM~~. natural mothering.

84. How Nat. mothers define "other" mothers.

86 NM critize others for paying homage to socially constructed ideas, ...they (also) fail to ~~ack~~ acknowledge the way in which their own idea are socially constructed. ...Um operate in a realm virtually untouched by social influence.

87. Roles "flow from bodies" (oversimplified in wording — my opinion)
Bobel says nat mothers say 5

the paradox: The paradox seems to be between feminist ideals: to be at home, mothering and not socially active outside the home vs. out of the home.

89. "Feeling" (Bobel is putting feeling, "knowing" and such feminine qualities as not-as-valid)

91: Bobel: NM "literally belong reason"

93. Bobel: "one wonders to what extent her self-worth is derived from her children's dependancy."

95. mothers felt that they must choose between demanding career or a good relationship w/ the family.

5 Resisting Culture, Embracing Nature

Natural Mothering and Control

97. The NM that spoke of choice also, at the same time, spoke of an indisputable logic of nature that compels them to live out their lives. They talk of choosing to live this way and also talk as if there is not other choice.

> Reexamine all you have been told ... dismiss what insults your soul.
> —attributed to Walt Whitman on Rad Mamas Discussion List

Contradictions are embedded in both the ideology and the practice of natural mothering. Scrutiny of what natural mothers do and say about what they do and say reveals one reality, but a different reality emerges upon deeper examination. One reality does not necessarily negate the other, however. Rather, the two realities seem to rub and chafe against each other, each one simultaneously informing, shaping, and challenging the other. In Chapter 4, I observe that while the natural mothers profess to *choose* their alternative lifestyle independent of conventional social pressure, they subscribe to a culturally constructed ideology of the body that determines their social practice. Their lives, it seems, are embedded in a paradox of liberation and constraint. I advance this notion of paradox in the present chapter. Having established the supreme rationale, if you will, for natural mothering, I will now interrogate some of the discrete ideological components of that rationale, the pieces that make up the whole.

104

Natural mothering struggles with the issue of control. Who controls mothering? it asks. Who controls families? Who, or maybe more appropriately *what*, controls mothers?

A key feature of natural mothering is its posture of resistance. Natural mothers rail against systems of control in the form of institutions and so-called experts. Tiny acts of rebellion fill their days. When a mother treats her child's ear infection with garlic oil instead of doctor-recommended antibiotics, she resists. She resists when she breastfeeds her three-year-old in the public library in spite of the disapproving gaze of those around her. When she ignores another school enrollment period or state-mandated vaccination date, she challenges the generally accepted norms of "good parenting." When she refuses to eat at McDonald's or buy her children Nike basketball shoes or a Disney sweatshirt, she makes a statement and positions herself and her children as "outsiders," even as rebels.

Characterizing her evolution from unblinking acceptance of social norms to critical evaluation and blanket skepticism, the natural mother seems almost smug in her self-analysis. She leads the enlightened life, she implies. She has come a long way, and now, proudly, she has arrived. "Before" she "bought into" the conventional thinking, "going along in the regular pattern," as one mother put it. "After," she is (relatively) free from the lure of materialism and deference to authority. Now less afraid to question, she boldly stands for every principle or practice that operates in the best interest of her family and her planet. But for all her resisting, challenging, and rebelling, she is not a true ideological independent, in spite of her claims. Rather, she redirects the allegiance others pledge to conventional authorities toward a more abstract but nonetheless powerful influence:

an ideology of the superiority of nature. She may be "turned off" by the hazards of mainstream culture, but she is "turned on" by the beauty, simplicity, and indisputable logic of nature. For her, nature provides the perfect model for healthy family living, and those who deny this are "out of touch" or, worse, brainwashed. While the natural mother resists mainstream culture, she embraces nature. Nature has become her new religion.

This chapter examines the tension between resistance and acceptance that I find central to natural mothering. First, I demonstrate how and why natural mothers find what they consider "mainstream culture" so inadequate and wrong-headed. By describing several "epiphanies" or processes of conversion, I show how particular interactions with conventional practices and institutions shaped their present stance as mothers who consciously operate outside the mainstream. Furthermore, once the mothers reject middle-class family lifestyles, they find themselves unwilling and unable to return to "doing things like everybody else," as one mother declared. Second, I investigate the ideology that natural mothers construct to replace their previous allegiance to normative lifestyle prescriptions. This ideology is represented by two touchstones seen by the mothers as definitive and irrevocable truths. The first, discovered by most of the natural mothers early in their parenting careers, entails "trusting/respecting nature." The second touchstone—"honoring the 'natural' bond of mother and children"—is put into practice by minimizing or eliminating mother-child separation (especially when the children are very young). In spite of critics who regard this hyper-attachment as excessive and dysfunctional, the natural mothers regard their connection as essential to child, family, and even, maternal health.

Resisting (Mainstream) Culture

Although some natural mothers portrayed themselves as "lifetime rebels"—people who, as one woman put it, "never have followed the strait and narrow"—a far larger number of women described a _process_ of awakening. Once they experienced some mainstream practice and found it lacking, this awakening gathered momentum and forced the mothers to challenge a number of conventional practices. This process, I was told, is on-going. The substance of these "epiphanies" is detailed below. Although each story is unique, they share a common denominator, which is a resultant distrust of and dissatisfaction with thinking and practices associated with mainstream culture. "Institutions are bad" is the dominant theme.[1] More specifically: Because institutions are detached from the natural world (and often created not to serve people, but to make money), they are flawed. Institutions (and the people who create and sustain them) objectify humans (and the environment) and have a myopic view of reality. Therefore, they cannot be trusted.

A majority of the natural mothers provided stories detailing negative experiences with what they described as "mainstream culture." Typically, as the tales unfolded, the narrators shook their heads as if to say, "Can you believe the stupidity of some people?" Frustrating and disappointing interactions with physicians, school officials, and daycare providers led many of the natural mothers to alternatives in health care, education, and childcare. Taken together, these epiphanies (or, more precisely, stories of disillusionment) demonstrate how natural mothers, individually and collectively, resist mainstream culture. Although I have arranged a sampling of these stories into topical categories, the interrelatedness of the topics merits emphasis.

A natural mother dismayed at her experience with institutional daycare typically denied that *any* institutional setting was appropriate for her children, including a conventional school. Mothers who shed their trust in and respect for medical doctors also became less trusting of other so-called authorities who prescribe appropriate modes of family care, such as popular parenting magazines (*Parents, Parenting,* and *Child,* to name a few) and childcare experts like T. Berry Brazelton and Penelope Leach. An undercurrent of skepticism flowed beneath each mother's story of discovery. And as each one questioned the validity of mainstream cultural prescriptions and practices, she searched for an alternative "truth," one more compatible with her changing world view.

Daycare   *what natural mothers think about certain mainstream institutions*

Several of the natural mothers—before they became mothers—had worked in or near daycare centers and spoke of "what it's like on the inside of those places." Once they got a "good hard look" at the reality of daycare, they told me, they were certain it was not the place for their children. Ellie Gluck-Kessler, homeschooling mother of Rachel and Crystal, had, as a student pursuing an education degree, worked at a daycare center considered the best in the city. Her experience there "impacted a lot" on her later decision to stay at home with her two children and forgo the career as an educator she had planned:

> I was really made uncomfortable by a lot of things we had to do. We had to take control, forcing kids into conformity, for the sake of the group, and things like that. That bothered me. Because at the time I was still working on this degree, this educational studies. And I thought that one of my ideas was

that I was going to open my own daycare center, and . . . I just kind of gave up on that idea.

Stacey Thurer-McReardon, homeschooling mother of three children and pregnant with her fourth, at one point worked outside the home while her husband, Rich, stayed home. Stacey glimpsed the interior of a daycare center while working in a social service agency with an in-house daycare facility. Like Ellie, Stacey did not like what she saw. She cited in particular the capriciousness of the daycare teacher.

> I realized I didn't want to go that route with my child. Because if you are on the inside of a daycare . . . the teacher was wonderful on some days and then moody and cranky and ornery on others. And as a parent looking in, I just thought, these kids never know what they're going to expect from this woman, you know, and I thought, I don't care what we have to do to our schedules, I just don't think it's fair to put a teeny little kid in from three months on. So I had . . . right away, even when I was real young—21—I thought a baby should be home, you know.

Education

Each homeschooling natural mother described a slightly different point of reckoning—the time she decided that conventional schooling fell short of her expectations for her children's education. Some women remembered being the "kind of kid that fell through the cracks in school" and wanted to protect their children from a similar fate. Others recalled feeling underchallenged—a problem they attributed to the "impossibility" that one teacher can accommodate 30 or more children with varying interests, temperaments, and aptitudes. Individuals need individual attention, the natural mothers concluded, and they believe that, as mothers, they are best equipped to provide that attention. Others, like Kim Monroe and Grace Burton (see Chapter 1), took issue with "externally imposed measuring rods of success." At home, they felt, their children could find their own mode of learning and flourish naturally without deference to peer pressure or teacher expectations.

Pat Lincoln, mother of two homeschooled boys, was repulsed by particular values taught in schools—values she felt were destructive, dangerous, and incompatible with her pacifism. When her first-born turned four and she began touring schools, the Persian Gulf War was at its height. Her observations at one school led her to rethink her original impression of homeschooling as something she couldn't possibly "add on," considering that she could "barely deal with the housework." A long-time peace and social justice activist, Pat was horrified when she observed first graders writing letters of support to a Gulf War soldier and reciting the Pledge of Allegiance in unison. "That was horrible," she told me. She abruptly changed her original view of homeschooling as "too hard" and committed herself to the task. Today she is an outspoken promoter of homeschooling's virtues.

Stacey Thurer-McReardon (the mother distressed by the unpredictability of daycare providers) was sensitive to criticism that homeschooling deprives the schools of active parents and children who could serve as agents of change, so she enrolled her two children in the local public school and joined the PTA. (Her story foreshadows the theme of Chapter 6, the social change potential of natural mothering.) Stacey described her attempts at "working within the system for change" as ineffective, and the experience led her back to homeschooling after one year. For instance, when she suggested that the PTA eliminate the prizes from the annual fair-fundraiser to save money and "make it a much realer event," the group of parents "just burst out laughing." She recounted a similar reaction when she suggested an alternative to fundraising for a new wooden playground:

> My experience was at the PTA. I was a crank. . . . You know, we talk about school ownership, why don't we have the parents and kids design and build the new playground? We could save so much money. We could get rid of this fundraiser and that fundraiser. And they said, "No." [And I said], "Don't you find it disruptive that not only are kids gone seven hours a day, but when they come home, they're often running back to school, doing spaghetti dinners or whatever? We don't have much time with our kids as it is . . . we want this good goal for the school, but instead of going directly for the goal, we do fundraiser, fundraiser, fundraiser." I said, "All those things take time, and what we're sacrificing is three evenings a month of dinner together, because, you know, you're just screaming in different directions." I said, "We've got to value our home life as much as what we can buy the kids for their school library." And again, it was just kind of like, "God, I wish she wouldn't have joined PTA." That's what I felt from everyone at the table. . . . I was totally ineffectual at changing anything, and I was actually just making meetings a lot longer and aggravating for everyone.

Stacey's "We've got to value our home life as much as what we can buy the kids for their school library" echoes a common concern among the natural mothers: the sacred space of the home as a refuge worthy of protection. Indeed, many mothers saw themselves as the (naturally selected) protectors of the home environment. Their job was to see that it remained a calm, warm, and nurturing environment for every family member. Grace Burton bemoaned the degeneration of the contemporary home into little more than a "dormitory" where family members sleep, bathe, and "might share food if they are lucky." In the interview quoted above, Stacey

[handwritten margin note: what is wrong w/ That?]

casts home life in opposition to material acquisition. Given a choice, she prefers fostering a healthy, connected home life to improving the school library. And, in fact, she did choose home over school when she decided *not* to reenroll her children in public school. When she made a commitment to homeschooling, she made a commitment to living outside a mainstream culture she saw as resistant to change.

These homeschooling mothers deem educational institutions inadequate; for some, like Stacey, who tried unsuccessfully to be a force for change, they are beyond repair. But the dominant systems of childcare and education are not the only ones found lacking. Reeling from unfavorable experiences with a "conventional, Western health care system" that failed to meet their needs, Helen Rector, Shannon O'Donnell, and others turned to alternative medicine. Their disillusionment with an institution they found inflexible, short-sighted, and arrogant led them to the conclusion that "there must be a better way." Surely, the search for a better way to live, one congruent with nature's dictates, is the essence of natural mothering. For many of the natural mothers, searching for the better way begins with discovering the "truth" about conventional life. The first step toward a natural lifestyle, then, is disillusionment with the status quo.

Health Care

Helen Rector had her first child in her late thirties. Now the mother of two boys, ages four and nine, and newly separated from their father, Helen has begun the process of reevaluating her life and finding her way as a single mother. When I asked her what originally led her to adopt an alternative lifestyle, she quickly referred to her interactions with physicians as members of the "modern, Western medical

system" that "didn't deal well" with her. They proved themselves, in her estimation, "grossly and totally inadequate."
She felt, for example, that her first miscarriage was treated
as inconsequential and insignificant because her physician
told her that miscarriages occur in 25 percent of pregnancies. Having miscarried a second time, she was further dismayed that her physician refused to investigate for
underlying causes until a third miscarriage occurred. The
"health care system . . . did not have very good information
for me. They had very . . . they had zero. They had no help
for me." Why couldn't the "system" regard her as an individual, she complained.

For her, the "system" erred in applying standard and
inflexible protocols that failed to account for individual differences. For example, Helen argued, she "was an older
mother who didn't have 20 years to figure out what was
wrong with [her] child." This interventionist attitude initially seems dissonant with natural mothering's usual hands-
off approach. But as Helen explains further, it is evident
that her notion of intervention does not step out of those
ideological bounds.

> It just seemed to me that there should be some basic things
> that you could do to help. For example, I was reading like
> crazy and I would call, and that was not taken well. For exam-
> ple, one time I called, and I could, of course, only talk to the
> nurse. I said, "You know, I'm just wondering if nutrition
> couldn't have something to do with this." And she said, "Well,
> I'll have to talk to the doctor." She called me back. The doctor
> didn't talk to me. And she said, "You know, the doctor said
> that nutrition has absolutely nothing to do with it, because
> women had babies in concentration camps, and their nutrition
> was just lousy." . . . It was so bizarre. And my response to it
> was, Look, I would not need a Ph.D. to know that nutrition
> has something to do with how a baby grows inside me. Please!

> It's like, Come on! Wake up! Smell the coffee! And that's the
> way I feel about a lot of modern Western medicine. . . . So I
> read voraciously, and that was my "in" into looking at health
> care in a different way. . . . Books are definitely best friends to
> me.

Helen's story is illustrative. The woman taps into a conventional system of care to meet a need, finds the care inadequate (and typically inaccessible, as when Helen's physician
was "protected" by the nurse), and turns away from conventional care to search for alternatives that take into
account "basic things" (read: natural and commonsensical)
such as nutrition, lifestyle, and state of mind.

Her story is especially provocative because it suggests a
key tension embedded in natural mothering—the tension
between taking and relinquishing control. Grieving over
her second miscarriage, Helen is poised to take action. She
is not satisfied with the explanation that miscarriages happen in 25 percent of pregnancies. She wants to *do* something about it. In other words, she is not willing to accept
passively the explanation that "this is natural and normal"
when it contradicts and distorts her personal understanding of natural and normal. Frustrated with a physician
who denies her own perception of what is natural and
normal, she wishes to wrest control from him and transfer
it to a medical perspective that recognizes the importance
of natural common sense. In other words, Helen wants to
take control *from* a (relatively new) tradition that she perceives as detached and impersonal and *return it to* an
ancient philosophy of health care that she perceives as
integrative and personalized. Believing that one doesn't
"need a Ph.D. to know that nutrition has something to do
with how a baby grows," for instance, Helen asserts her
own authority as an inquisitive patient. She reads vora-

ciously. She calls her doctor (even though her curiosity is "not taken well") and asks questions. She searches for the affirmation that something as basic as nutrition might prevent a miscarriage.

When Shannon O'Donnell, mother of a Waldorf kindergartner named Daisy, was diagnosed as having fibromyalgia, she, too, found conventional Western medicine lacking.[2] Her retelling of her negative experience bears a striking similarity to Helen's story, with overtones of sarcasm and frustration directed at mainstream medical practice and practitioners. "Western medicine, of course, has nothing to offer. Nothing. And I was just miserable. I was freaked out when I got [the fibromyalgia]. I thought, What am I going to do?" Having exhausted conventional resources, Shannon sought the services of an acupuncturist, who, she claims, saved her life. She also takes Chinese herbs, regularly practices yoga, and reports feeling almost no pain at all. She is grateful that she did not passively accept the dismal prognosis of conventional medicine, which promised her no respite from the chronic pain that accompanies her condition. Now, she "believe[s] in Eastern medicine a lot."

The World of Work

Perhaps the most significant body of "disillusionment stories" deals directly with the world of work. The natural mothers viewed paid labor outside the home as a dehumanizing experience that impoverished families and twisted priorities. Gabrielle Schulte, a born-again Christian and the mother of four children under five years of age, began her mothering career as soon as she left college. Our conversation turned to the consequences and possible sacrifices entailed by stay-at-home motherhood.

CB: Do you ever feel like you've lost anything by being at home?

GS: No. It's like you've lost your voice in the workplace, but what workplace?

CB: What do you mean, "what workplace?"

GS: I mean, what voice did you have in the workplace in the first place?

CB: Explain.

GS: Just, whatever, to share your ideas.

CB: As an employee?

GS: Yeah. But I think you can have more of an influence at home.

Like Gabrielle, Grace Burton regards the workplace as undesirable. Grace, who worked in accounting and finance for eight years, constructs what she calls the "outside world" as a force that runs counter to family solidarity, citing in particular the way the Industrial Revolution fractured families. One hazard Grace associates with immersion in the "outside world" is close-mindedness and lack of exposure to alternatives:

> When you are out of the home in the outside world, working, doing whatever it is you do there, those people are going to be less likely to be interested, open, and accepting of alternatives. They don't have any more time than you do, and where do they get off being better than me? If I have to wear the chains, you have to wear the chains, too. Whereas, being the person who is at home gives them some space, some time to think about those things, and to evaluate them.

Other mothers spoke more concretely of their observations of paid labor and its impact on family life. Janet Mitford is a devoted and outspoken stay-at-home mother to her homebirthed son. At age three, Gordon still breastfeeds throughout the day and night. Once a week, mother and son spend a day cooking and cleaning in another woman's home. This work (in combination with the child support she receives from Gordon's father) makes it possible for her to stay at home with her son. In the long term, Janet aspires to start a home-based natural fibers/natural dyes mail-order clothing business. Planning to homeschool Gordon, Janet recently joined the local homeschoolers' group and has begun making connections to facilitate her long-term commitment to Gordon's alternative and unschooled education.

But, like many other natural mothers, Janet had not *always* planned to live in this way. Rather, she had planned to chase a prestigious career in advertising to earn "the big money." But something changed her mind. Between earning a degree in advertising and having Gordon, Janet worked as a nanny for two years for a very career-identified couple. As she watched the sacrifices they made to earn generous salaries—in particular, the long hours and the separation from their child—Janet decided that she was not willing to "sell [her] soul" as her employers had:

> I saw how many hours a week they put into their jobs away from the house and at home, and I saw how they were living for the pursuit of money and status. . . . I realized I didn't want someone else to raise my children. And, in fact, once Andy, the father—and this surprised the heck out of me, because I didn't at the time really know that I was raising their son, and he said that I was. He said something about "When you have someone else raising your child . . ." And when he said it, I almost fell over backwards. I was like—! Okay, I didn't even know that, but you knew that?! You knew that?!

Janet's story is representative because in her view her choice went *against* her peers, peers she believes have confused their priorities. Tatiana Harding, mother of four daughters ranging in age from three months to 10 years, explained the impact of living next door to people she labeled "an unattached family." The parents "were gone and working so much that [she] wasn't quite sure where the parents fit in terms of their own role in the whole family." While the parents seemed inaccessible, the children's grandparents "were always there, always available," and for Tatiana "there was a dissonance in that," because grandparents are not a suitable substitute; parents should be "attached" to their own children. Later, when she planned her own family, she elected to stay at home, breastfeed each child beyond toddlerhood, and homeschool to ensure a mutually secure attachment with her children. And she declares that the lifestyle she chose is one she "really likes"—"No matter how hard some days can be, the joys come," Tatiana says with a smile and a sigh.

Stacey Thurer-McReardon's recounting of her own epiphany while her husband was unemployed for 10 months provides the most striking example of how a particular contact with the world of work reshaped a natural mother's view of the sphere outside the home. When Rich was laid off from his job as a human resources manager for a local hospital, the first thing the couple did was sell their newly purchased house. Desperately searching for work and unable to find anything, Rich slept about two nights a week, Stacey told me: "He was just going crazy [but] I was getting calmer and calmer, and happier and happier in a way."

> I . . . realized that all of these people were coming through for us. Every few days there would be some food delivered, or, I can't tell you the millions of ways, clothes dropped off for the kids. [Friends] would bring over breads and stews, and it just occurred to me how my well-being was not based on the money he was bringing in, because in this time of need, it was people who were getting us through, and if you have this sup-

port system of people, that's a million times better than a mil-
lion-dollar insurance policy, because people won't let you
starve if they are your friends, you know. . . . And my life just
seemed a million times simpler and easier, and I realized I was
happier. . . . I just realized . . . the security of a job is a false
security. It's the security of people that is the only true one,
and that was just emblazoned on me from that whole time.

Through the 10 months of Rich's unemployment, Stacey
discovered how a supportive community "got her through."
When Rich finally did find work, the Thurer-McReardons
continued to live simply and alternatively and do so today,
eschewing the false comfort that comes with the acquisition
of money and things—a mistake many conventional families make, according to the natural mothers.

Consumerism

For many of the natural mothers, consumerism is a key feature of what they regard as mainstream culture. Typically,
natural mothers perceive themselves as fervent critics of
American consumption practices. They assert that every
individual must make a pledge to live simply if the planet
and its inhabitants are to survive. Moreover, consumerism
sustains the capitalist system, which is increasingly dependent on mothers who work outside the home. When a
mother refuses to "buy into" the notion that her worth is
established by a paycheck or a job title, she performs an act
of resistance. Furthermore, when she is home, she is "freed
up" to construct a lifestyle less dependent on the goods and
services designed to assist overly busy people who do not
have time to cook, sew, garden, and build.

The natural mother not only affirms herself as the "naturally best" caretaker of her children (as explained in Chapter

4), but very consciously withdraws from a segment of consumer culture. <u>Because so many jobs involve the manufacture, promotion, and acquisition of goods, choosing not to have such a job destabilizes capitalism, these women believe.</u> According to this line of thinking, the spend-work-spend cycle is interrupted when mothers stay at home. A lifestyle distanced from popular culture creates fewer of the needs that would require more income, which would require more work for more pay. Natural mothers remove themselves from this cycle and live much simpler, less harried, more fulfilling lives.

Pat Lincoln, the social activist and mother of two boys who bristled at what she saw as an inappropriate show of patriotism in a first-grade classroom, spoke of her "very developed conscience that won't let me rest." She traced her dedication to simplicity to her organizing work:

> I remember somebody telling me about, or I found, that button, "Live Simply So That Others May Simply Live." I think I saw that and I got interested and I got one too. Through my solidarity work . . . I had been in Mexico and in Nicaragua and seen how very simply people live there, and I learned about how the U.S. population uses such humongous amounts of the world's resources, and I began to see how wrong it is robbing from those poor people. And then I learned more and more about the globalization of capitalism and how it's destroying all these old cultures and destroying ancient ways of life and ecosystems, and the way it's destroying is that it's drawing people into consumerism . . . and once you know that, how can you keep on buying that stuff and encouraging that?

And so for Pat, a simplified lifestyle is a political act. Consumerism is an "evil" to be combated, and one way of waging war against it is to stay at home and fashion a life that is only minimally dependent on goods and services produced by industries. The goal is a self-reliant, earth-friendly existence. There are neither televisions nor computers in Pat's household. The radio is off-limits to the children. Much of the family food is home-grown in a large organic garden; the balance is purchased at local co-ops or via community supported agriculture.[3] Pat and her family also participate in an upstart local program conceived as an alternative to participation in the cash nexus. Participants trade units of labor available: for instance, a freelance carpenter might supply one hour of repair service to someone who will, in turn, repay her with a one-hour massage. Pat is also very active in her local homeschoolers' group and in Creating Strong Families (CSF).[4]

Like Pat, Ruth Messner has been inspired by a highly developed environmental and social conscience to reform her consumption practices. While working on her doctoral thesis in medieval literature, Ruth separated from her husband, the father of her teenage daughter, Leah. The change forced her to evaluate her finances and spending patterns. It was then, she tells me, that she harnessed her finances and developed her "thrifty ways."

> I got in charge of my finances and I started learning what I was spending, and it occurred to me sometime, that was in the mid-eighties we're talking now, that if I buy things that I don't need that's using the world's resources in ways that are wasteful. So there was a long process of becoming attuned to our resources and waste in our lives. Monetary waste and the waste of the world's resources, those things go together. I crept into a certain environmentally sensitive and careful lifestyle, inch by inch, step by step, throughout the eighties.

In fact, Ruth became so concerned about environmental devastation that she wrote a (to my knowledge still unpublished) book that documents historical parallels to the current environmental crisis. She explains:

... because I really do feel ... that the earth is right at the crux point. We could mess it up and pull ourselves into a tailspin and go into a dark age that would make the one in 200, 400, 500, 600 A.D. look relatively benign, or because there is much deeper resource depletion than what they were starting with ... and I think how we act, what we do, is real important.

How we act and what we do are equally important to Kim Monroe, the mother of rural unschoolers Greta and Michael. Kim has pledged to lead a life as far removed from mainstream consumer culture as she can manage: "I always see things in terms of this grand scale, in terms of this balance. I feel that if people have excess, it's never far from the back of my mind that they're depriving so many in the world from having access to something else."

Pat's, Ruth's, and Kim's belief that each person needs to "live simply so that others may simply live" shapes a lifestyle where the mother is home providing intensive care to her children and enacting economical and sustainable modes of living. Disgust with consumer culture—a culture sustained by individuals who insist that they must work outside the home to earn enough to buy more goods—is at the root of many natural mothers' decision to eschew institutions and "do it themselves." These institutions include daycare, conventional schooling, health care, and the paid labor force, as well as practices of consumption—and somebody has to challenge them, say the natural mothers.

Once the mothers wrest control from mainstream culture, and in particular from the institutions that, in their view, pollute and diminish family life, they cannot let go of it, they tell me. A natural mother's knowledge is the source of her power, and she will not relinquish it. Armed with an array of negative interpretations of mainstream practices, such as the inadequacy of medical and educational institutions that sacrifice individual needs to the efficient functioning of the group, the natural mothers exercise their own sense of personal power and agency. But at the same time they take control from (mainstream) culture, they return it to nature, pledging their abiding respect, trust, and honor to its "indisputable" logic.

When Helen Rector insisted that "there must be something that can be done" about her miscarriages, she enacted her own sense of personal agency, wresting control away from her physician and taking it for herself, only to hand it over to nature. As the natural mothers surrendered to the power and, in their view, the promise of nature, they seized control from a dominant culture that they perceive as running counter to their parenting agenda. As people distort inherently natural processes, alternatives become necessary, they say. And once they experience the alternatives—"coming home" to the way "things should be"—it is difficult, even impossible, to go back. Helen Rector compared the process of rejecting dominant, mainstream ideas about parenting and family life to lifting sheets off her head. Gesturing over her head as if liberating herself, she analogized:

> Until you realize the sheets are there, you are incredulous when someone points it out to you. What do you mean there is a sheet there? But once you get rid of it, you are amazed at how clearly you can see, and it all makes sense. But the thing is, once you start removing the first sheet, you realize there are more, and it just goes on and on.

This process of infinite enlightenment emerged repeatedly in the discourse of natural mothering. The mothers spoke of the interconnectedness of alternatives—the way one practice opened the door to another and another, virtually without end. When I began my research, I was intrigued by the overlaps in alternative family life. What was the common denominator among such a wide variety of practices? What does homeschooling your six-year-old have to do with baking your own bread? Why are the women in La Leche League International the same women who volunteer at the local food co-op? What does a midwife have in common with an unschooler?

Complicating these questions were apparent disparities in the politics and backgrounds of many alternative practitioners. It is not uncommon to see born-again Christians and self-described radical feminists in attendance at the same La Leche League meeting (and, indeed, there are both in my sample). And midwives catch the babies of both Amish women and college professors. When I queried the natural mothers about what they thought united these populations and practices, I heard a common response: We all distrust institutions and resent being told what to do. Certainly the groups listed above subscribe to some social dictum—all social groups do—but it may be true that a shared distrust of conventional authority marks the homebirthing mothers, the organic farmers, and the leaders of La Leche League. Doing it yourself and doing it pure and simple—this is the universal credo of the natural mother, regardless of her other associations. And once the natural mother reclaims her authority from the local school board and the medical community, she is unwilling to give it back. Ingrid, the Christian homeschooling mother of four children, explained: "I realized—as soon as you take on the responsibility for homeschooling, you go from passive to active; things that you let other people decide, all of a sudden you have to decide. Everything that's going to happen to your kid is determined by you; you know, it's like this big responsibility."

This evolution from passive to active was common to all of the women with whom I spoke. Some made the adjustment swiftly; others struggled with it for years. Ultimately, each of the natural mothers admitted to a key conceptual shift that brought her to her current mothering practice—embracing nature and resisting culture. The characterizations of contemporary culture, often expressed as "the mainstream," the "rest of the world," "conventional life," or simply "out there," constructed a nature/culture split wherein nature is good, pure, untarnished, and wise, and culture is bad, dirty, crass, greedy, and naive. "Other" mothers were implicated as sadly duped by a corporate, capitalist economy that prescribes material gain as the solution to every problem ("the bad other mothers" in Chapter 4). "If other mothers only knew what *we* know," the natural mothers say (with varying degrees of pity or disdain), "they would value their own naturally given talents to nurture their families with little more than breasts, arms, and a warm, healthy home environment."

Natural mothers fault naive first-time moms who are regularly lured into hospitals thinking that state-of-the-art medical technology will assure them a virtually pain-free, uncomplicated birth. They berate parents who send their children off to expensive schools that boast a computer workstation for every student, convinced that better resources translate into a high-quality education. Given these strong sentiments (and harsh judgments), it is no surprise that the bad, materialistic, and repressive "world out there" holds little appeal for natural mothers.

But if mainstream culture is rejected, what is accepted in its place? Sometimes it was easier to establish what the natural mothers *did not* believe than what they *did*. Still, our conversations unearthed a complicated answer to this question in the form of two key "lessons" of natural mothering, which are described in detail below. Natural mothers regard their experiences with mainstream culture as educational and transformative, and so are their newfound understandings of what "mothering really means." For most, the progression from a typical "mainstream mom" who patiently subscribes to society's dictates to an "alternative mom" who "takes nothing for granted" (as one put it) was a slow evolution marked by a series of disillusioning encounters with mainstream culture, as documented above. But it is not enough to implicate mainstream culture in the production of social ills and family disintegration—surely many people have an arsenal of similar tales of disillusionment. I am not asserting that natural mothers stand alone as critics of contemporary society. What distinguishes them from other mothers and from other social critics is their abiding faith in nature. The following section explores this faith in nature in depth by looking closely at the "lessons of motherhood" that demonstrated to them the power of nature.

The Lessons of Motherhood

Lesson One: Respect and Trust Nature

One of the most arresting themes that emerged from our conversations was the assertion that mothering itself teaches mothers, in specific and profound ways, that they have little control. The mothers spoke passionately of the importance of "taking mothering back" from institutions and experts; then, having regained control of mothering practice as detailed above, they spoke eloquently of the futility of resisting nature.

Stacey Thurer-McReardon, the 32-year-old mother of three who was pregnant with her fourth when her hus-

band experienced 10 months of joblessness, spoke of out-
growing her need to "tweak things," opting instead to
respect what she regarded as the natural course of growth,
change, and development. Over time, she told me, she
learned that life's crises—sick children, marital problems,
financial issues—eventually iron themselves out when left
alone. When her kids complain of feeling ill, she insists that
they simply go to bed: no aspirin, no worry, no call to the
physician. "Just go to bed. Sleep is the best thing for you,"
she tells them. "Give your body a chance to rally." Ingrid
Kitzinger, mother of four, former Peace Corps volunteer,
and devout Christian, described Eve's experience of birth as
a metaphor for how mothers learn their powerlessness yet
are empowered through nature to mother appropriately:

> [Eve] was given childbirth, and so she learns about what it's
> like to have your body taken over by something else. . . . And
> you go through the whole childbirth thing, which you don't
> really control; it just sort of happens to you. You just have this
> happen to you. I think that gives you an analogy. Then you
> have this little baby come, and you have to somehow or other
> relate to this baby. You have to really focus in and try to learn
> about what this little person is, each one being so different.
> And yet the baby is programed to respond to you because they
> hear your voice. It always amazed me with Alan. I mean,
> here's this kid, I know nothing about being a mother, and
> when I pick him up, he stops crying, and it's kind of like: Kid,
> if you were smarter, you wouldn't do this, because I don't
> know what I am doing (laughter).

This "knowing" and surrender

When the mothers spoke of nature, they spoke of a
monolithic and static concept, the one true thing that pre-
dates humankind and remains pure and unadulterated. To
them, nature is the perfect model for human behavior
because it is separate from and unpolluted by human
manipulation. This view, of course, is problematic; it denies

denys
The
many
ways
nature
is
culturally
constructed

the many ways in which nature is indeed culturally constructed and thus dynamic (see, for instance, Cronon 1995
for a sampling of this view). While there is a nonhuman
world beyond the human imagination, it is hard to deny the
human role in perceiving, naming, prioritizing, and analyzing nature. Landscapes, for instance, are designed by both
humans who create boundaries around them and by nonhuman forces (which can be and often are shaped by
humans as well). As Anne Whiston Spirn reminds us:

> All landscapes are constructed. Garden, forest, city, and wilder-
> ness are shaped by rivers and rain, plants and animals, human
> hands and minds. They are phenomena of nature and products
> of culture. There is always a tension in landscape between the
> reality and autonomy of the nonhuman and its cultural con-
> struction, between the human impulse to wonder at the wild
> and the compulsion to use, manage, and control. (1995, p.
> 113)

Nevertheless, the natural mothers do not regard nature
as culturally constructed; in fact, its separation from culture
is what they find so attractive about it. In their view, nature
is powerful because it is pure and charged with a logic
beyond human reason. It is so powerful that it wrests control from the individual.

Cheryl Ferraro, an art school graduate, also wrestled with
this issue of control. She spoke of her progression from
being a self-centered and naive expectant mother to her
current awareness as a child-centered and informed mother
of two teenagers and two very young children. Somewhat
sheepishly, she described her attitude toward mothering
while pregnant with her first child as evidence of how far
she'd come. Ignorant of the demands on the mother of an
infant and convinced by her college psychology textbook
that newborns sleep 16 hours a day, Cheryl was disap-

pointed to learn that the daycare center she called would not take babies until they were six weeks old. She was incredulous: "Six weeks old! But they sleep for 16 hours! Can't you take them sooner? What am I gonna do for six weeks?" As for finding a family physician, she remembers asking a stranger at a yard sale for a recommendation. Luckily, the physician provided satisfactory care, but she shakes her head in amazement that she approached health care for her family with such recklessness.

Once her new daughter arrived, Cheryl found herself "panicking over every little thing." In particular, her daughter's insatiable desire to nurse day and night overwhelmed and worried her. She called her La Leche League leader and exclaimed, "Something is wrong. This child is malfunctioning!" Eighteen years and three children later, Cheryl and I sit together talking as she contentedly and patiently nurses her six-month-old son, unconcerned about the length of his nursing sessions. She is confident that she is equipped to meet his needs and spends little time worrying that something is wrong, or that something must be changed. She contrasts her mothering experience then and now:

> Well, I suppose just in general my feeling from the first baby to this one is so different. Because with Shari . . . I always had a feeling of, When's this going to be over? When am I going to go on to the next thing? When am I going to get my time off? . . . I have had the light at the end of the tunnel. I know that it does end eventually, so it's not as if . . . not that kind of nervousness. Like, maybe I better take charge now, and take the reins, and say how I want this to go and stuff. And it was that kind of feeling. Whereas after you get over that, then it's more like, yeah, yeah, it will happen when it happens.

Another key dimension of this first "lesson of motherhood" is the importance of trust. For the natural mothers, good mothering practice is predicated on *trusting* that nature will resolve all parenting dilemmas. Perhaps the simplest, most direct statement came from Claire Thompson, home-schooling mother of four children, who said, "I trust in the process of life." When a mother is concerned that her new-born is sleeping too little and nursing too much, she need only trust that all is as it should be, and she will relax. Babies are "programed" to sleep and eat when they need to, and a mother need only trust this natural logic—this is the founda-tion of natural mothering. When a child complains of an ear infection, the natural mother resists the cultural mandate to rush to the family doctor and request antibiotics. Rather, she trusts the child's own immune system to fight the infection. It may take longer for the ear infection to pass, but it will pass, the natural mothers assure themselves and one another.

Similarly, the homeschooling mothers speak of trusting their children and themselves to provide a proper educa-tion. The cardinal rule of homeschooling—and in particular unschooling, I was told—is, "Relax, relax, relax." An unschooling/homeschooling family trusts that a natural inquisitiveness and thirst for knowledge will guide a child to experience life, and for these families experiential, interest-driven learning is far superior to conventional educational methods. "Kids will get what they need when properly sup-ported and encouraged" serves as the general guideline, and parents simply act as facilitators. Ingrid Kitzinger, who began homeschooling in the 1970s when the U.S.-based secular homeschooling movement was in its infancy, summarized her educational, trust-based philosophy: "I think if you give them enough time, those things come together, and they do learn about those other things as well. But they've done it at their pace, in a way that makes sense to them, and they are used to the idea, they've learned about themselves and their interests, and they've also had a chance to develop a style of learning so that it's something that they continue to do."

Sally Mitsuhashi, strongly identified with cultural feminist ideology and the divorced mother of two grown daughters, spoke passionately about the centrality of trust in mothering. She saw a trust-based style of parenting as particularly gendered:

> [Conventional parenting is] based on fear, and I think men are much more fearful in their approach to life than women. They're not nearly so trusting, and like [the medieval mystic] Julia of Norwich wrote, "All shall be well again." And that's just a woman's approach, "Oh yeah, this is rough, but it can get good." And it's just a much broader approach. So I guess— and (her daughter) pointed out that I was actually feminist to the core for all those years, mainly with my level of trust, and whatever I was presented with: "Well, we can fix that, we can work with that." And looking at many alternatives—that's a woman's view of seeing many ways of working at something. And the other thing is, it doesn't have to be fixed right now. A sense of time. And the other is nonlinear. Male is so linear from here to there, and woman is more spiral.

Sally's description of the differences between men's and women's ways of seeing (cf. Belenky et al., 1986) is wholly consistent with cultural feminist characterizations of gender differences. For Sally, a mother is endowed with the ability to see holistically. This holistic vision is open to alternatives and thereby free from conventional constraints that prescribe one authority-approved way of managing parenting challenges. Interestingly, Sally's discourse links trust with feminism: The fact that she harbors a certain confidence that "all shall be well again" qualifies her as a feminist (an identification confirmed by her daughter). She is the type of feminist who trusts women's way of seeing and interacting with the world and perceives it as superior to men's.

[handwritten note:] ↑ does she feel it is "superior" To men? oR different Than men?

The thread that weaves through the mothers' stories of trusting nature is the recognition that when you trust, you can relax. And when you relax, you can let nature take control. You may as well, the natural mothers tell me; after all, you don't have a choice.

Lesson Two: Honor the Natural Bond of Mothers and Children

The second lesson revealed through the discourse of the natural mothers deals directly with the nature and quality of the mother–child relationship. This relationship, they maintain, fuses mothers and children virtually into a single entity, an extension of the relationship during pregnancy, when the child is wholly dependent on the mother for survival. The natural mother recognizes no artificial, socially prescribed division between mother and child. Rather, they operate as one bonded unit. Everything the child needs is provided by the mother. With her breasts, she provides food and immunity to sickness. With her arms, she provides comfort and safety. With her voice, her experience, and her own curiosity, she provides stimulation. Together, mother and child (or children) create their own self-supporting universe. It is this understanding of the closely woven mother–child relationship that the natural mothers use to deflect the criticism that they are sacrificing their lives to their children. When Sally Mitsuhashi, for example, was asked if her lifestyle ever felt unnecessarily sacrificial, she responded confidently:

> I never felt like it was a sacrifice. It is, but it was not a negative sacrifice. I had friends who asked me, you know, "How can you just keep sacrificing your life for these children?" And to me it was never negative, because it was a gift to them, and the other thing: *I didn't feel that separate from them.* That I did something for my children, it was actually doing it for me, too.

It wasn't like, I'm having no fun in this world and I'm doing everything for the children. I remember we would wake up in the morning, when Melanie wasn't in school, and we would say, "Well, let's see, what do we do today? Shall we go down to the lake, or go to the woods and kick in the leaves?" you know? "Well," she'd say, "I want to go to the lake." So I would pack up the baby and her, and we'd go down to Lake Michigan. We'd sit an hour while they threw rocks in the lake. Now, to me that's wonderful. I could sit and meditate on the lake while they had their fun . . . to have left them somewhere and gone and done something else that didn't satisfy like this. It was a beautiful time of nurturing myself at the same time I was nurturing them. [Emphasis mine.]

In Sally's view, maternal self-sacrifice is not the problem; a culture that casts mothers and children in opposition is. She has a label for the pervasive view that mothers and children are continually at odds with one another in the pursuit of disparate needs:

That's the adversarial role of parent and child, and it's still being encouraged, this adversarial role, with the pediatricians, because they have a lot of input into the childrearing, and I hear them talking about, and I've read some of the books that say, "You really must have a life of your own and not give over to your children, because then you're sacrificing, you're not being people yourself." And that makes it adversarial—that you can't give to your children and give to yourself at the same time.

Bobel
slumming
natural
Mothering

Among the serious repercussions of the merged mother–child identity at the root of natural mothering is the way it marginalizes fathers. Over and over again, I heard women describe a household division of labor where the mother took almost complete responsibility for childcare. In the most equitable arrangements, the father assumed responsibility for some portion of home care; but he was always the primary breadwinner. This struck me as puzzling, given the feminist orientation of many of the mothers as well as the claim that parents of both genders are equally important to a child's well-being. But when I pressed the mothers to say why they, as women, were the designated stay-at-home, intensive parent, explanations based on biological difference surfaced yet again. Thanks to the supreme importance placed on breastfeeding, mothers seldom shared infant feeding with fathers or other potential caregivers. Over time, these feeding norms established caring patterns that persisted throughout mothers' and fathers' parenting careers. When the mother is established as the singular food source and, furthermore, when nursing is the sole source of emotional security and comfort, the mother is constructed as irreplaceable. An irreplaceable mother has a great deal of power. Nevertheless, some natural mothers spoke of feeling overwhelmed with their responsibilities. Michelle Jones-Grant admitted that she did "all the work with a newborn."

> I had kinda talked him [her husband] into having a second child. He let himself be talked into it and agreed to it, but wasn't wholeheartedly committed to it, because one of the things that I said was, "It's no trouble for you. I do all the work with a newborn. You know, it doesn't even affect your life." And all of a sudden, I'm like, "I need help with this baby! I need help with this baby! Please help me!" We had this argument. "What's the matter with you, anyway?" [she finally said to him.]

Fathers in this study can be imagined along a continuum of helpfulness. One father offered to do all the family grocery shopping (until his wife offered to assume the task in exchange for his agreement to have a third child—another bartering-for-baby scenario).[5] Some fathers shared preparation of the evening meal. A few fathers took exclusive responsibility for diaper changing and diaper washing when possible (but since most of these men worked outside the home, their contribution to total diapering labor was small). Among the least helpful dads, some performed no child- or home care activities at all. Theresa Reyes described her husband as "companion for me, financial provider, and TV-watcher."

Several women, like Jeanette Zientarski, homeschooling mother of two girls, disclosed frustration with husbands who "checked out" upon arriving home to a house full of children and household demands. In the 17 households that had televisions, excessive TV watching was often cited as problematic.[6] During one interview, Tatiana Harding, mother of four children including a newborn and a very demanding special-needs toddler, attempted to juggle the children's demands while carrying on our conversation. While she performed this Herculean feat, her husband (whom she described as "in a lot of ways more alternative than me") relaxed in front of the television in the basement. Was this typical, a prearranged division of labor? Would he have helped if she had directly asked him to? Was she annoyed by his failure to lend a hand?

Mary Schwartz offered a reluctant but nonetheless enlightening comparison of her first and second husbands, revealing the difference involved fathers can make. Mary was forced to relinquish her intensive mothering practice when she suffered a debilitating back injury. Although she tried to breastfeed her new baby, her condition made that impossible. So Dad stepped in and served as primary caregiver, forever altering their parental division of labor. In Mary's view, this alteration was "for the best," deepening the bond between baby and father, liberating Mary from the sole responsibility for childcare, both practically and psychically, and permitting her to nurture herself in a way she was unable to in her first marriage.

> I know that the first time around it was always me who noticed anything that Cliff was saying or communicating to us, and I would get resentful that my husband wasn't seeming to appear to pick up that quickly on it. This way, I think George would have been sensitive to it if he didn't understand it, but just the fact that he was reading her [the baby's] mind, all the ways that she was communicating . . . And he's just as quick to help her out.

George recently agreed to take their six-month-old daughter to visit his parents. Mary had originally planned to make the trip, but then decided that she would like a quiet weekend to herself. She could count on his willingness to act as primary caregiver:

> I told him yesterday that I really didn't want to go [away for weekend], and I was really afraid that he would discount that, but he really understood, and that meant so much to me. I felt guilty after I realized it was okay with him. I felt guilty, thinking I'll be away from Lilith overnight, but then I think I will weigh my old way of thinking. I would have never left Cliff overnight, but now it is just so apparent to me how much I need that time, and it makes me feel very good that, if she cries or something, that he'll be right there. It's not like I felt previously. I don't mean to keep comparing marriages here, but I felt previously that I was the only one who could take care of my son.

Mary's story is exceptional. For most natural mothers, the familial division of labor is very traditional: Mother assumes the care of the private, home-based sphere, including home care and childcare, and Father assumes responsibility for the public sphere, namely breadwinning. A number of women struggled with this arrangement, but none spoke of attempts to alter it. For women convinced that a mother is endowed with a natural connection to her children, first through pregnancy and later through breast-feeding, this division of labor is "inevitable." Mary Schwartz's story shows how some rupture that alters the division of labor can reveal this "inevitability" as the product of determinist constructions of gender.

Another aspect of the inextricable mother–child bond is the notion that not only do children need mothers near and always accessible, but *mothers need their children* to meet their own daily emotional needs. The latter dimension is popularly regarded as a taboo subject, inviting criticism of overidentified mothers who use their children in morally and psychologically suspect ways. Nevertheless, with characteristic boldness and unconventionality, the natural mothers discussed their own attachments to their children as a way of explaining the persistence of their commitment to intensive parenting even beyond the initial days and weeks of mothering a newborn. Ingrid Kitzinger related her views in an extended monologue:

> I think we [women] have a need to mother. Once you have the child, you have a need to be near your child. I think you have a need to touch your child and to hold the child. I thought I was doing it with Alan all the time, and yet when he was ready to move away, the mother has to also be ready to move. And it's like, "Oh, I haven't held him quite enough yet." And I feel really sorry for women who have their children in daycare, who aren't able to do the actual holding. Because it's like, you . . . they . . . we have developmental stages for children. I think there are developmental stages for mothers and that you have to go through it or else; and if your child is progressing and you're trying to hold him back because you're not done . . . yet, or sometimes later on in your life, I see these women trying to teach their kid to be independent, and

they're pushing him away, and they're pushing him away, and they're: "You have to learn to do this, like sleep in a bed or sleep all night, you have to do this, you have to do that." And it's like, "No, no, no. You don't understand. You guys have to go through this together, and when you're both ready, they can move on. And then it's healthy . . . you're both ready." But if the child is ready and the mother isn't, she's pulling back on him. And if she's done—she's not really done, but if she thinks she's done—she's trying to push the kid and he's not really ready, it's like trying to make him walk without letting him crawl. It's not emotionally. . . . This is my feeling. I haven't read that anywhere, but that's my feeling.

According to natural mothering, a healthy family is an attached family, a family where children are kept close and identities overlap. Take, for example, the way Ingrid represented the fusing of the identities of mother and child. As she searched for the correct word, she began by speaking of "you" (the mother), then shifted to "they" (children), and ultimately settled on "we" (mother and child).

Kim Monroe echoes this view. She confesses that because she needed to keep her young son close, she resisted the social norm when the time came to send him off to school— just as she challenged feminist ideology as a college student by her intense desire for motherhood (see Chapter 4):

And at the time when Michael became school-age, it just did-n't feel right to send a child that young off to school. . . . My child might have been ready to go to school, but I wasn't ready. I felt that that would be absolutely taboo for any women to admit. I was aware of that aspect to it. . . . I think it took the same degree of courage to make a statement like that as it would have for me to admit my interest in mothering back in the seventies.

Claire Thompson applied this notion of mothers needing children to weaning: "[My son] was an early weaner by [La

Leche] League standards. He was like two and a half when he weaned. Oh my God, my baby weaned. He's so young. How could he do it? And he did it to me! How dare he take that away from me?"

Referring to a later stage in the mother–child relationship, Grace Burton took issue with what she considers the unnecessary separation of teenagers from parents (and younger siblings). Teens, she said, "need to be a part of our lives. We have created a subculture of people called teenagers, schoolkids in general, but particularly teenagers, and it annoys me immensely. They are a part of our society. Why is it that they cannot do what the rest of us do? Why do they have to be separated away from us?"

Again and again, I heard women speak of their reluctance to separate from their children, resisting this division for *their own sake* and condemning the cultural norms that expect it. Is natural mothering child-centered or mother-centered? The women are armed with defenses of their attachment to their children. They have been criticized countless times by people who see their relationships with their children as unhealthy or signaling some familial dysfunction, and they are weary of the judgment. Claire Thompson, explaining her desire to remain at home with her large family, burst out: "I am not co-dependent. *I think it is in my nature* to be a hearth-and-home kind of person. It was just in my nature to be that caretaking person. I don't think I am co-dependent" (emphasis mine).

Who or what built up Claire's defenses? Has she been publicly challenged before? Claire clearly attributes her lifestyle to her "nature." Yet I wonder if she is compelled to defend her decision to remain at home (for her, less a choice than a calling) because she is *not* altogether convinced that an unusually close relationship with her children is in the

it can be hard to "convince" yourself Because the mainstream culture is so unsupportive

best interest of everyone involved. Claire's example demonstrates not only some potential ambivalence about the hyper-attachment characteristic of natural mothering, but the centrality—once again—of explanations based on nature to natural mothering ideology.

Here too the ideology of natural mothering wrestles with the issue of control. The natural mothers deem "mainstream" culture a force that is overly materialistic, insensitive to individual needs, and generally repressive. Ultimately, "mainstream" culture is to be avoided as much as possible. Claiming to be freed from the control of culture, the natural mothers present themselves as rebels distanced from the pressures of conventional life. At the same time, however, they embrace an understanding of nature that renders them virtually powerless and almost completely dependent on a male breadwinner. In this chapter we expose a contradiction at the heart of natural mothering. "Going with the flow" and "letting things happen naturally" are preached as the safest, sanest way to parent. Nature is an omnipotent but benign force to trust, respect, and honor. To do otherwise is to invite family dysfunction and environmental devastation.

The natural mothers can hardly be said to assume a passive role as they construct their mothering style. While they embrace a natural parenting ethic, they simultaneously reject norms of conventional parenting dependent on expert advice, institutional rules, and corporate marketing. As the natural mothers cultivate a respect for natural, organic processes, they foster a disdain for the products and processes associated with culture. Paradoxically, the natural mothers simultaneously resist and embrace the dictates of forces larger than themselves.

6 Natural Mothering

Social Change or Narcissistic Retreat?

We have explored what natural mothers do and why, but an important question remains: Can natural mothering effect social change? In *Recreating Motherhood: Ideology and Technology in a Patriarchal Society* (1989), Barbara Katz Rothman conceptualizes American motherhood as "rest[ing] on three deeply rooted ideologies—capitalism, technology and patriarchy." Each of these constitutes a "way a group looks at the world, a way of organizing our thinking about the world." Regarding the three ideologies not as separate, but as more like the "strands of a tightly woven braid," she nevertheless defines the parameters of each as together they shape American motherhood (1989, p. 26).

Ideologies of Motherhood

The Ideology of Patriarchy

"Women's reality is not the dominant ideology, and women's view of the world is overruled by men's view," Katz Rothman states succinctly (1989, p. 27). Situated in a patriarchal context, motherhood becomes "what mothers and babies signify to men." Motherhood is constructed as a service to men; babies are men's property. Mothers themselves, as women,

141

exercise little personal agency. Katz Rothman delivers these examples of motherhood under patriarchy: "For women this can mean too many pregnancies or too few; 'trying again' for a son; covering up male infertility with donor insemination treated as the deepest darkest secret; having some of our children called 'illegitimate'; not having access to abortions we do want; being pressured into abortions we may not want" (p. 27).

In a patriarchal system, children are established as being born to men, from the bodies of women. In this system, men's seed is planted in the bodies of women, who then bear the babies of the men who impregnate them. All humans are the products of men's seed; women simply carry men's babies. That is, patriarchy is rooted in the act of impregnating. Even when women's role in procreation is acknowledged, it is seen through the lens of this idea of seed. "The central concept of patriarchy, the importance of seed, [is] retained by extending the concept to women" (1989, p. 36).

The Ideology of Capitalism

Katz Rothman defines capitalism simply: "Goods are produced for profit" (1989, p. 27). Prior to the transition to a capitalist system, the family operated as a unit of production, making goods for its own consumption and, later, for barter, trade, and sale. When the Industrial Revolution restructured the economy and, in turn, the family, the family became a unit of consumption. One consequence of this transition was the commodification of children. As commodities, children were something to be possessed, something to be exchanged, something that held a market value. The sale of black-market babies represents perhaps the clearest contemporary example of this ideology in practice. By extension, women's function as progenitors is commodifed.

In the capitalist system, women neither own nor control the products of their own labor. Katz Rothman suggests that the "commodification of children and the proletarianization of motherhood" is the consequence of this ideology. "We are no longer talking about mothers and babies at all—we are talking about laborers and their products" (1989, p. 66). Capitalism (at least in the United States) is so entrenched in our collective consciousness that, she observes, "we think of the profit motive as if it were a basic human desire, greed as if it were part of human nature" (p. 67).

The Ideology of Technology

Finally, the ideology of technology shapes motherhood by encouraging "us to see ourselves as objects, to see people as made up of machines and part of larger machines" (1989, p. 28). In short, the ideology of technology suggests a mechanized view of human beings and human processes, including, significantly, the experience of motherhood. As Katz Rothman states, "The ideology of technological society is more than this package of tools, gimmicks, know-how. It is a way of thinking about the world in mechanical, industrial terms" (p. 49). This ideology drives a view of the mother as a mechanical entity. In *The Woman in the Body: A Cultural Analysis of Reproduction* (1987), Emily Martin shows how childbirth is seen as production and women's bodies as factories churning out babies. And if women's bodies are like machines, then they can be improved, tweaked, and calibrated, and the processes associated with them can be predicted and controlled. Birth is medicalized; labor, in particular, is managed. And when breastfeeding does not "work," the baby receives a scientifically derived, laboratory-produced product in place of mother's milk. Technology interacts with motherhood, and the outcome is a mother better than the one nature designed.

Patriarchy, capitalism, and technology simultaneously inform one another, shaping our social understandings of motherhood. This influence extends to mothers themselves, natural and otherwise. Katz Rothman argues that the effect of the three ideologies has been to split motherhood apart, forcing it into a series of dysfunctional dualisms: mind and body, public and private, personal and political, work and home, production and reproduction, masculine and feminine. (Her book, she writes, "is about the ways we can put motherhood back together again" [1989, p. 89].) And although the natural mothers might not use these words, they, too see themselves as participants in this rebuilding effort, as pioneers who resist a male-centered, commodified, and mechanized conceptualization of motherhood. They offer culture, simply through their example, something different.

Most of the natural mothers viewed their lives as strategic missions to effect social change. "I've decided that absolutely everything I do is political," Grace Burton stated emphatically. Pat Lincoln is recognized within the membership of CSF as a person who consciously evaluates each lifestyle choice for its social impact. Her garden was organic before it that was fashionable; she unplugged her television before children's viewing habits became a topic of popular controversy. When a group of CSF mothers gather to discuss the "right thing" to do or not do, buy or not buy, it is not uncommon for someone to ask, "What would Pat do?" Because of her reputation, Pat has become an informal clearinghouse for socially conscious information. While I was visiting a natural mother who was having a set of wooden steps built to her side door, the carpenter approached her and suggested a particular sealant to finish the job. The mother asked about the chemical makeup of the product. Although the carpenter assured her that it was nontoxic and safe for children and the ground water, she was dubious. She called Pat. Sure enough, Pat had information about sealants and was able to direct the mother to an alternative product (much to the displeasure of the carpenter, who had to chase down a less readily available product).

While women like Pat and Grace see their family lives as consciously political, some of the mothers I interviewed offered a political analysis only when I probed a bit. When I asked, "Would you consider your life political in some way? Is the way you mother a social statement in any way?" they typically responded as Robin Johnson, mother of four children under five, did: "I hadn't thought of it that way, but, yeah, my life is indeed political."

The most striking thing about the paradigm of natural mothering as a politicized lifestyle is the specific way in which it is realized. Rather than taking to the streets, running for local office, or dedicating their lives to grassroots community organizing, these women strive to effect social change through the day-to-day practice of mothering outside the mainstream. Janet Mitford summarized this position: "In reality, when you figure it's a real radical thing to raise your children and instill the values that you can . . . instill feminism in the[m], and you can do a lot more to shake up the system by staying home with them."

Michelle Jones-Grant depicted motherhood as a noble enterprise endowed with a unique potential to alter the sociocultural landscape:

I feel like the most important job that I do, no matter what I end up doing with my life—the most important job that I do is going to be raising my children. That's the thing that's going to have the most impact on the world, that's the thing that's going to give me the most satisfaction in my life, that's the thing that if I do a lousy job, it's going to be doing the biggest disservice to humanity. That's the thing that, if I do a good job, might be the best thing that I can do as a service to humanity, even if I go on to do research and come up with a cure for some horrifying disease. That maybe could rival doing a good job raising kids. But, you know, anything else that I do probably won't.

Theresa Reyes cited an example of consumer-driven childbirth reform when she argued that "taking care of doing what we think is right" can effect long term, large-scale social change:

Like, for instance, I had my first three [babies] at St. Joe's, which was terrible as far as support of natural birth and even breastfeeding. Okay, my fourth baby was had at Christ Hospital, and they were so supportive of natural birth, and so supportive of breastfeeding. It's like they read a La Leche League manual! And if women like us were not demanding that, no hospital would be doing that. . . . So, in that respect, us doing that does push practice.

political

For Chris Johnson-Fairchild, "mothering differently" is a project of micro-level social change akin to what missionaries call "witnessing": living out a particular set of values to set an example of a preferred life. Witnessing is part of the work of a missionary. While striving to convert members of the host community to a different (and, they argue, superior) religious belief system, the missionary also witnesses to the same community a life lived according to those spiritual and moral precepts. If one believes that individuals are best persuaded by the subtle yet powerful example of their peers, the act of living as you wish others to live is arguably a missionary's most powerful tool. Chris drew on her three-year tenure as a lay Maryknoll missionary in South America:

> CJ-F: See, the Maryknolls begin their witnessing by how you live, and I try to, and it's hard for me, because I'm not activist, but when we were living in Paraguay, Jim [her husband] would say, "It was like a big part of what you're doing, Chris, is being a mother, is living in a marriage that's different from their marriages. You're out and about. Like they're noticing that." Just doing your wash, and it's like . . . Okay (sigh). Because I felt like, Why am I doing this? I could be doing something, but, you know, this witnessing by just how you live. There, for sure, people were watching me because of the fishbowl thing. . . . Here, I don't know. I think it does make people a little uncomfortable, maybe. Like our neighbors here and the people at church, they're real curious about homeschooling, and . . .
>
> CB: So it's a real subtle social change?
>
> CJ-F: Yeah. Yeah. Yeah. Yeah.
>
> CB: Slow?
>
> CJ-F: Yeah, and I like revolution. It's more exciting . . . being a part of something bigger. Sharing that.

Chris and others like her, frustrated with the slow process of legislative change, put their faith in living by example, like missionaries in a strange land. As one woman put it, "My life is a mission." But, as this passage reveals, witnessing lacks excitement. Chris seems uncertain that witnessing is "enough." It is "not activist." Without her husband's encouragement, would she have persevered? Yet Chris's ambivalence was unique; other mothers expressed confidence in their life-as-mission. Certainly not all mothers adopted the mission paradigm in so many words, but most of them adopted it in spirit and spoke of their mothering practice as radical, life-changing, and potentially revolutionary.

But why choose this approach? If revolution is a goal, why not employ more conventional methods of social change? Where are the rallies? The letter-writing campaigns? The protests? What soured the natural mothers on organized social-change efforts? What led them to the conclusion that they could be most effective as "missionaries in a strange land"? The natural mothers decided, each in her own time, that micro-level social change offered the best chance at making a difference in the world. For some this decision was rooted in disillusionment with larger-scale efforts; for others, it was rooted in a sense of personal urgency. They cannot wait for society to change.

Stacey Thurer-McReardon's story of working in the local PTA during her children's year in the public schools reveals the former theme—disillusionment. Grace Burton never felt the tug of community responsibility as Stacey did. She was clear early in her parenting career: "I just didn't have the time to wait for the system to figure out how to do it right for my child. . . . I didn't have time to do that. . . . It's my child we're working with here!" Many of the natural mothers shared Grace's family-centered perspective and consistently and unapologetically put their individual families first.

As the natural mothers discussed their lives as having the potential to alter the social landscape in meaningful ways, I remained dubious. I did not doubt the sincerity of their commitment; certainly I understood how using cloth diapers mitigated the landfill problem, and supporting organic farming improved water and soil quality. Yet questions of efficiency remained. It is exceedingly difficult to measure success or failure even in traditional social movements. It is even more challenging to evaluate phenomena like natural mothering because there is no easily discernible "enemy" or centralized form of power. At the same time, I began to question the importance of privilege in natural mothering and wonder if it was tied to romantic-seeming notions about the roles of natural mothers in effecting change.

Do You Have To Be Rich To Be Responsible?
Natural Mothering, Privilege, and Exclusivity

simplify ... hire a maid
—Inscription on sweatshirt advertised in *Signals: A Catalog for Fans and Friends of Public Television* (1998)

Jeanette Zientarski spoke of mothering as "changing the world." She argued for an instinctual basis for social-change-driven mothering (and fathering), the intuitively derived practice beyond the scope of rational choice analyzed in Chapter 4:

> JZ: I think it's instinctual, is it not, for mothers and fathers to raise their kids in a way that they think will better their kids, that will give them a good place, a good springboard, from which to jump?

> CB: Then why isn't it instinctual for everyone?

Jeanette met my question with a silence that supported the analysis advanced in Chapter 4. The natural mothers "just know" what is in the best interest of their children, and when probed about *how* they know, they stare blankly. It is a feeling, a gut-level awareness ... it can be neither described nor analyzed, they told me, implying that my question was the wrong one, that I just didn't get it. But how can it be that some mothers operate on instinct while others do not? If we are all endowed with a human instinct that flowers into a mothering instinct once we become mothers, why aren't all mothers aspiring to be natural mothers? If naturally dyed organic cotton sleepers are "naturally" the right clothing choice for babies, then why aren't such garments more widely available? Or at least in heavier demand? If breast-feeding your baby "felt right" to every woman, why do formula-fed babies far outnumber breastfed ones?

The demographic profile of the women I interviewed for this study may help to answer these questions (see Appendix, including Table 1).The characteristics of the 32 women at the center of this inquiry, including age, marital status, occupational history, and education, reveal a privileged population. All the informants were white, and all appeared to be heterosexual. Eighty-eight percent were married. Eighty-seven percent owned their own homes. Two-thirds of the husbands were white-collar professionals. Eighty-one percent of the women had attended college, while 69 percent had completed a degree. A full 53 percent spoke of significant and often extended travel experience, including living abroad and missionary work, a statistic I find most interesting and revealing. These demographics do not reflect the general population. Clearly, these highly educated women have access to resources as wives and home-owners and enjoy the prestige that accompanies their sexual and racial statuses.

The demographic homogeneity of the women interviewed is not accidental. And as much as a small, nonrandom sample can reflect a larger population, this one does. For instance, in Juliet Schor's (1998) survey of 800 American adults, of the 28 percent whom she identified as "voluntary downshifters," 69 percent had at least attended college (a full 25 percent had completed a four-year degree), and 85 percent were Caucasian. Her sample departs from mine, however, in the area of income. Although I did not collect precise

[handwritten margin note: Actually not all make that much money]

income data from my informants, their husbands' occupations suggested income levels that would situate many of them comfortably in the middle class. In contrast, a full 30 percent of Schor's sample earned between $10,000 and $25,000 annually, suggesting that voluntary downshifters had not previously enjoyed a large measure of material comfort. A subset of Schor's downshifters—her "simplelivers"—may match the income levels of my sample more closely. According to Schor, in contrast to downshifters, simple livers "transcend [the] trade-off" between time and money by establishing a low-level sufficiency income and living within their means; living beyond that point, they believe, is destructive, to self, family, community, or planet (p. 138). Although Schor claims that her subset of simple livers is too small to be representative, she observes that simple livers tend to be middle-class whites with at least a college education, and that they are not and never were poor in a more abstract but nonetheless meaningful way:

> Simple-livers can [simplify] because they are rich in cultural capital . . . and in human capital (economists' term for education and training). Some started with hefty bank accounts or homes of their own. Because they tend to be at least middle-class and well educated, they are able to manage the world around them. They have social and personal confidence, know how to work the system, and have connections to powerful people and institutions. Unlike the traditional poor, they have *options*—including the option of jumping back into mainstream culture. (1998, p. 137)

Natural mothers (a subset of simple livers) enjoy a privileged position in which their alternative lifestyle is possible. That is, it is *because* they enjoy a secure economic status, solidified by their racial, educational, and class status, that they can afford to take the social risks involved in non-

mainstream practices. In this sense, their privilege serves as
a sort of safety net, protecting them from a nasty fall should
they, for instance, be challenged for nursing their toddler in
a public place or refusing conventional medical treatment
for an illness. Being white and middle-class, they are less
likely to come under attack. A poor woman of color spotted
breastfeeding an older child could risk censure and certainly
judgment. A mother receiving state benefits is *required* to
vaccinate her children; waiving vaccinations is not an
option. An immigrant woman known to use herbal remedies to treat illness risks a scolding by her family physician.

disagree

In addition to the safety net, access to resources figures
prominently in the enactment of natural mothering. Natural
mothering is expensive. Organic foods, for example, are
costly: Organic produce costs considerably more than conventionally grown foods. Homeopathic and herbal remedies are not covered under insurance plans, so a family that
opts to use an alternative medicine has to pay the costs out-
of-pocket. And certainly stay-at-home motherhood, a key
feature of natural mothering, requires the economic security
afforded by a wage-earning partner. These economic factors
are not lost on the natural mothers themselves. Mary
Schwartz, for example, expressed annoyance at the cost of
providing what she considers the best for her family:

disagree

disagree

> I went to [a natural foods grocery store] yesterday and I love—
> you know it just opened up on the East Side now . . . but I get
> so annoyed at Whole Foods because it's, God, if everyone had
> the money to spend there. There are always people who can
> buy the very best organic food. They can take care of them-
> selves the very best way, and their kids. And there are others
> who have absolutely nothing, you know; it doesn't feel right
> . . . this sort of idea that "This is my family, this is where it
> begins and ends here."

Mary's comments demonstrate a sensitivity to the real price tag associated with natural mothering, along with a self-consciousness about the kind of family-based narcissism that "begins and ends" with "This is my family." She sits uneasily with this realization.

When I asked Chris Johnson-Fairchild why natural mothers were predominantly white, middle-class, and married, she replied:

> CJ-F: I think it takes money. That's my opinion. We have to be able to be home. Single parents can't do it. I don't think so. I don't think they could. I know a woman from church who got divorced, and she was homeschooling before, and she sent her kids back [to school]. She was crying a lot during the day, and she thought, "Maybe it would be better for them if they were in school." It takes money to eat well. That's one of my things with organic food, is that it's so expensive. I told Jim I can't justify, I'm not convinced enough, I'm not a believer enough, to spend that much money on pears. Every once in a while, but I couldn't buy a bag of organic pears and pay that much. It's expensive. It is expensive.
>
> CB: But isn't [Voluntary Simplicity] supposed to be *frugal* living? Why does it remain . . . ?
>
> CJ-F: Don't you think it makes a difference that it is voluntary for us?
>
> CB: That we once had access to the resources and now . . . ?
>
> CJ-F: . . . and we know we could, if we wanted to. . . . We have a safety net. We have education. We could get a job. We could get a good-paying job if we wanted to. It's a choice. It's a choice—you know the difference when you don't have a choice, and you're living tight like a tightwad, and I would resent it. But when it's a choice . . .

Again, we hear the discourse of "choice." Carrie Dittmer similarly invoked the importance of *choosing* simplicity when she attempted to make sense of the privileged status of natural mothers. Comparing her own upbringing with her husband's, she wondered if natural mothering, especially the Simple Living component of the lifestyle, is reserved for those who "had it" once and chose to let it go. When I probed, she mused:

> You know, I hadn't thought of that before, but . . . that people are making a conscious choice because it's like, "Been there, had that." My husband desires more prestige [*sic*] things than I do because I think he heard a lot—his mother died when he was 13, and I think he heard a lot, "Well, we can't afford that, we can't afford that," growing up. And so he ends up feeling poor in situations where I feel like I'm choosing to feel poor, be poor . . . so he always felt different in a way that he didn't want to be.

Theresa Reyes agreed that natural mothers are privileged women, pursuing a lifestyle that may be designed only for the few:

> How can I be breastfeeding this baby when my husband is not around, except to beat me up . . . ? We do have privilege. We have the luxury of just concentrating and taking care of that baby. Of course, look at me. When I had my baby, my husband couldn't speak English and had a job as a janitor. But then again, look at the maturity, the mental resources we had to work with, which a person who didn't come from a good family life . . .

Theresa does not see her husband's class position (and, by association, hers) as a determining factor. Rather, she cites the couple's "maturity," "mental resources," and "good family life" as the raw material that allows her to be a natural mother. Education and "good" upbringing are more important than economic status, in her view, demonstrating yet again the natural mothers' tendency to emphasize the power of family over structural realities in the shaping of individual life experience. Similarly, Mary Schwartz maintains that natural mothering is for only a select group:

> MS: I think we are the people that can afford to be choosy about what we want for our kids, and that bothers me that it's that way. I don't like seeing this as an elitist sort of thing. But it can be, and everyone I know who's doing it is married and white. Yeah. It bothers me.

good question

> CB: What's it gonna take for it to become more accessible to different kinds of people?

good answer

> MS: I think just for . . . the whole sense of families to realize that they have the skills to teach their kids. . . . I really wish that. I think that if parents would be able to stay at home with their kids the first two years, they would realize how important it is, and it would be an impetus for homeschooling. They would see that it doesn't just stop there.

Natural mothers enjoy not only the economic benefits of their social class, past and present; they also enjoy a secure social *status*. Backed up by their racial, educational, and class capital they can afford to take social risks and practice nonmainstream activities. In this sense, their privilege serves as a screen against public censure as well as an economic safety net.

Perhaps the strongest evidence of the centrality of privilege to natural mothering is the resentment of the less privileged natural mothers. Cheryl Ferraro, who has struggled financially, remarked with a touch of anger: "I have at times, when I've been really financially strained, seen other people and thought, well, sure, it's easy for them to say, 'Do XYZ with your kids,' because they've got a husband that is making a $100,000 a year. Why shouldn't they be saying that?" This intra-group tension highlights the awareness of some natural mothers that privilege precedes natural mothering.

Is this true?

Betsy Morehouse spoke of the common ground shared by natural mothers as cracked down the middle, divided between those with privilege and those without. She, poor and single, placed her young son, Liam, in daycare so that she could work full-time. The facility required all children to nap after lunch, a policy Betsy felt was inappropriate and insensitive to the individual needs of children. She removed Liam and enrolled him at a different daycare, only to find that it, too, required all children to nap. "There's nothing I can do," Betsy remarked, and her feelings of helplessness turned to resentment and anger as she described the rift between herself and the more privileged natural mothers:

> Sometimes, I get really angry, because I feel . . . like all the pro-
> ponents of La Leche League . . . are partnered women who are
> pretty comfortable. And like at times I've felt like, "Fuck you,
> all of you. You have no idea, you have no idea, how hard it is
> to make those kind of decisions. Yeah. He's in daycare." Well,
> it's funny. Middle-class women or partnered women, like
> sometimes will assume things about—if you're an alternative
> parent, you're doing this—and for me, like if I absolutely can't
> do that, because I don't have the money, I don't have a partner,
> I feel like I'm not as conscious of a parent, and I don't like that.

So is natural mothering an elitist and exclusive practice? Is it reserved for those who can afford to purchase 100 percent organic cotton, vegetable-dyed baby clothes and natural shampoos, lotions, toothpastes and deodorants at twice the cost (at least) of more conventional and more widely available products? Is natural mothering *practically* possible only for those who can afford to stay home, nursing, baking, sewing, and gardening? The answer to this question is fundamental to understanding natural mothering, and more specifically its capacity to evolve into a social movement of significance.

To find the answer, I probed in a variety of ways. I saved these more direct questions for the end of the interviews, when it appeared that the informant had "told her story" and was looking to me to provide some structure to the interview. I asked the mothers if they could describe a "typical" natural mother, or, put differently, describe the characteristics that link the women who adopt natural mothering. I reasoned that a loose, insider-derived profile of a natural mother might not only yield demographic information, but also suggest how the natural mothers saw themselves as part of a larger whole—and whether they held an understanding of natural mothering as dependent on some measure of privilege. The results were varied and interesting:

I've always said that it's people that are suspicious of popular culture, and suspicious of materialism. I don't know if you can narrow it down any more than that. (Kim Monroe)

Maybe the mom is somebody who's attuned to the sense of natural—attuned to what's best for herself and her baby on a more natural level. Somebody who's not afraid to face, I don't know what the word is, what appears to be sacrifice for the sake of herself and her baby . . . [someone who is willing to] question the rules and face their, yeah, question the conventional wisdom, like, "Why suffer pain in childbirth? Take something for it. Have an epidural. It's okay. It's standard medical procedure." I suppose you would have to at least question it or think about it to come to a different conclusion. (Theresa Reyes)

I think a strong sense of self would be the one thing that would jump to mind, because there are some more talkative, and some that are quieter, and some that are leaders, and some that are followers. But I think a strong sense of self, of, like, what you think is important, or what you think is right, rather than kind of just going along with what's normal . . . of not just taking things at face value, but maybe having a questioning sort of attitude. And saying, "Well, what's the best practice here?" And being willing to be the only one with that point of view. (Carrie Dittmer)

Jenny Strauss, the childbirth educator, offered a profile of her alternative childbirth students as representative of natural mothers in general:

A lot of the people I work with come to me because my classes are marketed towards women who are educated and taking an active role in their lives. So the people I get tend to be educated. . . . So my typical student is somebody who's often used to taking an active role in their life. They're often into alternative health care already, have taken responsibility in that area of their life. So taking responsibility for the birth just follows through from that. They often describe themselves as information-seekers. They just sort of have that culture of, "Oh, this is new! Let's find out what we can about it." . . . They're readers, and they have access to other information . . . they are in general information-seekers. They're also in general people who are a pretty high percentage of, sort of, independent professional kinds. High percentage of self-employed, or if not self-employed, at least they're pretty autonomous in their profession. [They say,] "I hate people telling me what to do" . . . pure learning people, you know, off on their own, charting their own path, researching what they want to research . . . people who are thinkers. They don't like, "So you do it this way because you do it this way."

What spoke loudest in these narratives was what was not said. The natural mothers' profiles categorically omitted a discussion of privilege, especially the type attached to class, marital status, sexual orientation, and race. Theresa and Jenny noted the importance of education to independent thinking and doing, but the informants on the whole did not seem sensitized to how important cultural capital is to the implementation of natural mothering. The importance of skills and connections as well as the practical and social confidence to get needs met seemed to evade them. One feature of privilege is ignorance of it: For instance, Peggy McIntosh conceptualizes white privilege as an "invisible knapsack" one carries around virtually unconsciously (1989, p. 10). So it seems for the natural mothers. Might their very omission of privilege validate its importance? For them, what distinguishes natural mothers from more conventional ones is "a strong sense of self," a suspicion of popular culture, an enduring quest for information and pure knowledge, and being "attuned to the sense of natural." Judging from these accounts, anyone can be a natural mother; the only requirement is a certain mentality or world view.

Knowing the demographics of my sample of 32 informants, I was not satisfied that it was mere accident that the women were exclusively white, almost all college-educated, married, and apparently heterosexual and middle-class; it seemed implausible that they were connected merely by a "questioning attitude." So I tried another probe, and this time without subtlety. Did they wonder if some women were more inclined than others to be natural mothers? Could the way society was set up have something to do with who was a natural mother and who was not? All of my informants were intrigued by this question, responding with comments such as, "Boy, that's a good question . . ." And their answers were varied. Some had already entertained the notion that natural mothering was reserved for the privileged few, but their notion of privilege was often narrow. Theresa Reyes, who had earlier argued for the centrality of education, reiterated that point: Clearly one main thing separated natural mothers from more conventional ones, and that was formal education:

> I think educated people tend to be more flexible in their think-
> ing. They tend to weigh alternatives more, and evaluate and

analyze before doing things. That's just a benefit of education, for everything. So, therefore, they are more likely to say, "Should I bottle-feed, should I breastfeed, what is best for my baby?" And analyze and come to conclusions. Just because that's a characteristic of educated people.

But when I probed further, asking if perhaps something more abstract, such as the way society is arranged and structured, may make it easier for some women to adopt the practices of natural mothers, she mused:

> Maybe the structure of our society does make it hard, except for women of privilege, who are educated enough to be motivated and have the option to stay near the babies often. That's why it's too bad [federal welfare] reform makes women go back to work so soon. It would be nice if there could be a medical exception for those breastfeeding.

Kim Monroe also made the link between privilege and natural mothering. Reflecting on her associations with Hispanic women who, through their commitment to work and wage earning, demonstrated middle-class aspirations that precluded stay-at-home, intensive motherhood, she recalled: "I knew quite a lot of Hispanic women because I worked in a deli for a while where a lot of them would work. And they would work up until the moment they gave birth because money had tremendous priority to them, because earning money meant, I think, an opportunity to really have a chance for their children to belong to the middle class."

Mary Schwartz turned to the content of *Mothering* magazine as exemplary of the elitism of natural mothering—a quality she became acutely aware of when she was separated and divorced:

> To me, [*Mothering* has] become a sort of yuppyish sort of thing, like all the products are so expensive, and it just seems like an

elitist thing. And I get annoyed with the homeschooling things about this elitist group of people that do the very best for their children. I get that feeling from there. And then I want to be sure that we're thinking about everyone's children. . . . When I was separated and divorced I felt like, from the magazine I didn't feel as much support.

Mary's awareness of the context of privilege in which natural mothers operate is unsettling for her. As she talks, she grows agitated, vacillating between expressions of hopelessness and disgust. She connected her critique of natural mothering as an elitist practice to a related critique of natural mothering as the narcissistic retreat of the privileged. More colloquially, some natural mothers worried that natural mothering was a social "cop out." Mary, for one, expressed weariness with homeschoolers who relentlessly criticize public school systems while injecting no energy into their reform:

> I felt that it's important for Cliff [her son] to help out with the neighbors, just to get to know everyone. I can understand that criticism [of homeschooling as selfish] because I think in a lot of cases it is a valid one. We can't just—I hear things about public schools, and people are so critical sometimes of public schools. I think it's really a cop out to just criticize them and not become involved with the kids in some way.

But Grace Burton, expressing a much more common sentiment, explained her choice to retreat *instead of* reform: She did not have the assertiveness or the time to change the system (see her comments in Chapter 1):

> GB: You know, people said, "Well, why don't you just work within the system?" I didn't have time to do that.

> CB: Do you hear a lot of that criticism . . . by pulling your children out of school and by choosing to birth at home, the system will then persist and no change will occur?

GB: Especially the school system, that was a pretty common comment. People seem to fear you're taking out the best kids with the parents who would be most involved and leaving the school system with the problems. The school system is the problem. Our society may be the problem, but I don't think that that's *my* obligation to try and fix them at that point. . . . My family comes first, and that's what we need to focus on.

Chris Johnson-Fairchild, who had earlier expressed ambivalence about micro-level social change, echoed Grace's thoughts:

I had been a fighter within the system, and I've seen systems sometimes change. But they don't change permanently, you know. They get a new principal or—I worked in the schools for 10 years, which is one of the reasons why homeschooling appealed to me. I've been there. The best schools, and they weren't any good. . . . We sort of left the Catholic church; we go to an Episcopal church now, because I'm tired of doing call to action and just dah dah dah dah. But you know, sometimes you just want to pray, you just want to find community, and be nurtured by that and don't struggle. It is easier, I think, to do it at home. It's easier. You can control it. You don't have to fight so hard. [If one of her children decides to go to school] I'd have to be up at the school, have to volunteer for this and that, and try to dah dah dah. And I don't want—I would much rather put my energy here, and so it's sort of like a cop out, because it could make a difference for the 20 other kids in the class, if I would help out in the classroom, give the teacher some space—probably could.

When I asked if caring for other children—in particular, the children who attend her neighborhood school—was her social responsibility, she replied, emphatically, yes:

If we don't . . . I'm a believer in the community, in taking care of others, and reaching out. So, to some extent, like [the local homeschooling group] and CSF provide—but to the extent that it's closed, I'm uncomfortable with it. It's only—it's one of the things about CSF that Jim and I got uncomfortable with. We're all so self-focused and looking inward and helping this one do this and this one do that [members helping one another]. Well, if we have all this energy, why not turn around and do outreach? . . . We feel some commitment to go beyond the boundaries, and I think we're all incredibly gifted in that group, and to just sit with your gift and wallow in it, so to speak, makes me uncomfortable.

Yet Chris and the other natural mothers do not focus their energies on macro-level social change, but on their families. Whether they are disillusioned or impatient, they have elected to apply themselves to the project of natural mothering. And this project, they believe, can and will reshape motherhood; it will fulfill Barbara Katz Rothman's desire to "put motherhood back together again." But will it? Can it?

Putting Family First and Mom Last: Natural Mothering and Accommodating Patriarchy

Natural mothers wrestle openly with the ideologies of motherhood identified by Katz Rothman, naming them, challenging them, pushing against their boundaries. But their success is uneven. As they resist cultural prescriptions of good mothering practice in the areas of daycare, health care, education, work, and consumerism, they tug at the intertwined threads of capitalism and technology. When they repeat La Leche League's "people before things," they take a stand against materialism, and thus the capitalist commodification of human experience. When they refuse to hook their soon-to-be-born baby to a fetal monitor, they invest their trust in natural processes that they consider superior to and separate from processes mediated by technology.

Yet the natural mothers do not resist patriarchal constructions of motherhood. While they make the fairly radical claim that female productivity must be ascribed social value, they do not resist the most fundamental assumptions about what it means to be a woman in the contemporary age. Natural mothering, rooted in biologically determinist understandings of gender, reifies a male-centered view of role-bound women. The "natural" in natural mothering may liberate mothers from a mechanized and commodified experience of their maternity, but it reproduces a gendered experience that subordinates their needs to those of child and husband and models that experience for their children.

Like the female moral reformers who predated them, these women embrace a politics of accommodation. Like the maternalists who "used" their femininity to persuade men to take them seriously as moral role models, the natural mothers push the boundaries of their role while embracing specific features of it. While they resist certain capitalist and technological structures and attempt to wrest control from institutions and "experts" they perceive as threatening to the best interests of American families, they do not challenge the structure and content of gender relations. Because the very ideology that underwrites gender goes unchallenged, their push for societal validation for traditional female productivity remains nothing but a wish.

Natural mothering, then, adapts to patriarchal notions about women and men, including, very specifically, the gendered division of labor and, more abstractly, the dualistic split between private and public spheres and the preeminence of biology as shaper of human destiny. It accepts a standard that rationalizes women's inferior social position. Natural mothering, consistent with its historical tradition of female moral reform, is a lifestyle that is simultaneously rebellious and obedient. It resists, but not too much.

7 Conclusion

> We are finding our way back home, not by erecting a bigger and more idealistic edifice of family, but by collapsing into what family has always been. A place where we can fall apart. A place where the worst in us can act out, where we can suck our thumbs, where we can hide in the bathroom. Family is the place where the strangest people live, a place where we can hold onto one another and come in from the cold.
> —Peggy O'Mara, *The Way Back Home* (1991, p. 139)

This book has explored a style of parenting that reclaims nature and the home—a "way back home." The "way" refers to the path along which natural mothers travel toward their destination: the home-based, nuclear family nurtured by Mother and Mother Nature. As the natural mothers enact a way of living that recalls an earlier era less dependent on technology and commercial culture to meet family needs, they go "back." Although the precise "way" differs for each mother, similarities range across the sample I interviewed. It was those similarities, categorized as paradoxical themes, that drove my examination. Each woman offered her own analysis of contemporary culture and the impoverished condition of conventional parenting. And, in response, each woman volunteered her own rationale for choosing a labor-intensive, child-centered lifestyle—that is, for finding her way back home. For Peggy O'Mara, founding editor of *Mothering*, the way back home is "about finding our way back to valuing the family, to valuing relationship, and finding our way back to ourselves from which all of our relationships stem" (1991, p. 6).

165

When I began this project in the mid-1990s, I used the term "natural mothering" to capture an ideological and practical coherence that I thought I sensed in a particular style of parenting. At first, I simply intuited the existence of a growing movement of women embracing and promoting an antidote for divorce rates, teen pregnancy, uninspired education, and chronically ill children. Natural mothers believe that families go wrong when they "buy into" commercialism and materialism and forget the beauty of nature and its power to guide human practice. The healthiest families, they argue, live simply and employ time-tested ways of meeting basic needs. Breastfeeding, consuming whole foods, and avoiding technological forms of entertainment and communication will reverse many of the destructive trends they find so troubling. "Turning our backs on nature" is the "cause" of many grave societal and personal problems; embracing nature again is the solution.

At that time I had to seek out natural mothers aggressively and comb the shelves for periodicals and books that reflected the set of values that, I believed, informed their lifestyle. Today the search for "evidence" would be less arduous. Recently I received two pieces of mail that demonstrate just how ubiquitous the ideas associated with natural mothering are becoming. First, my long-distance provider, which has begun suggesting books for summer reading, recommends *The Whole Parenting Guide* by Alan Reder, briefly described as: "A practical and inspiring guide to holistic parenting written for all parents who want to promote the growth and well-being of their children's minds, bodies and spirits while improving their communities and their planet as a whole."

I suspect that more women than men will pick up that book. And more women than men will agonize over whether their parenting style falls short of "improving their communities and their planet as a whole."

The second piece of mail was a brochure recruiting Voluntary Simplicity group facilitators in my community (an area, I might add, not known for its progressivism). Earlier in the year, an organization called "Earth Connection" offered a series of workshops; now, the organizers are looking for interested people to "help to make this movement grow." These two small examples—and I have many more—suggest that simple living, Attachment Parenting, and their hybrid, natural mothering, are gaining wider cultural appeal. Whether the ideas translate into practice, of course, is another matter. But at least the ideas themselves seem to carry a bit more currency than they did just a few years ago when I began noticing the growing popularity of organic produce and baby slings.

If natural mothering is indeed growing in popularity, our ability to evaluate it takes on greater importance. Does currently available social movement theory provide the tools to examine this movement and others like it? In other words, are social movement theorists equipped to understand phenomena (like natural mothering) that do not precisely fit the definition of a social movement? Contemporary Social Movement theory conceptualizes collective identity narrowly: as a group of people with shared values and vision banding together to effect change (see Taylor and Whittier, 1992, p. 105). Implied in this definition is the presence of physical community—individuals who know one another and work together toward some common goal. There is a clear sense of *we* drawn from knowing precisely who is *in* and who is *out*. The strength of one's association with the group may vary, but there is clearly a group.

Natural mothering seems to deviate from this model. Most of the natural mothers operate independently. Apart

really?

from the members of Creating Stronger Families (CSF), the natural mothers base their lifestyle not on a group ethic, but on a closely held system of individual values. For most natural mothers, the sense of collectivity that exists is generated by reading periodicals and books such as *Mothering* magazine and Jean Liedloff's *Continuum Concept* (1985). Some mothers felt strongly that their many related choices fit into a larger whole, a movement of other mothers doing the same. But some were not so sure. One mother's frustrated cry—"If this is a movement, where are my sisters?"—captures their sense of disconnection. They feel a part of *something*, but what?

During the course of the interviews, many of the mothers wondered aloud with me: Is natural mothering a trend? An ideology? A parenting style? A movement? And who else is doing it, whatever this elusive "it" is?

Social Movement theory needs to account for nonconnected people who build a movement. In the case of natural mothering, I found that information alone, through texts and computers, attracts and compels people to action. Lack of collectivity did not prevent natural mothers from participating in a form of social action. How, then, can we theorize about disparate individuals living out a similar lifestyle and creating change in their everyday lives? How do we understand a movement that lacks rallies, groups, even small clusters of people connecting and validating each other's activism? When individuals in different places make the same choices for the same reasons, is this a movement? If these same people are exposed to an expanded range of choices and "know how" by others they never meet or even interact with, are they still engaged in some kind of community? A community directing its energy toward social change? In this information age, perhaps it is time to develop theoretical models that help us detect the creation of community via text—in the form of both printed word and online communication—and understand how this elusive sense of community can support individuals acting on a social agenda, as in the case of natural mothering. In addition, we need to develop ways to measure the impact of such communities.

[handwritten margin note: What kind of feminist lens did Boael use?]

In any case, we must examine all such efforts at social revision through a feminist lens and question the promises and prescriptions for social change. When examining a nascent movement (or an established one), it is prudent to ask, "How does this affect women?" "What does it mean for women?" Recall the haunting diary entry of Abigail Alcott, who wrote, "There was only one slave at Fruitlands, . . . and that was a woman" (Shi, 1985, p. 137). When considering any new prescription for the enlightened life, it is imperative that we ask: Who are the ideologues and who are the practitioners? More specifically: Does back-to-the-land mean back-to-oppressive-gender-roles? When we resist change, do we risk romanticizing the past and obscuring the fact that some technological advances have reduced some burdens and risk for women, people of color, and the poor?

Directions for Further Study

In addition to suggesting a closer look at New Social Movement theory, this research highlights other salient areas in need of further study. At this point, we know something about the why and what of natural mothering from the point of view of the mothers themselves. What about an in-depth study of their children? How do the kids turn out? Do they fulfill their parents' hopes that they will be more independent, connected, and peaceful? Does homeschooling actually produce brighter, more creative, and more confident adults?

A body of data is accumulating on the effects of homeschooling, and it appears that by some measures homeschooled children fare quite well.[1] But can that success be attributed to natural mothering in general or to some particular aspect of it? Does eating organic foods, giving birth at home, breastfeeding for several years, and avoiding conventional medicine have a measurable (and positive) outcome? Furthermore, do the children of natural mothers adopt the values of their parents, becoming, as self-avowed "pioneer" Claire Thompson hoped, the "settlers" of this new movement? Without a systematic study of the children, we cannot know.

Similarly, a study of natural mothers as empty nesters should yield interesting data. Consider Sally Mitsuhashi, whose two grown children both returned home to live with her. Is this typical of the natural mother's household in later years? Throughout these pages, my informants have invoked the incredible bond between mother and child, forged and painstakingly massaged by the mothers. What will they do when the children reach an independent age and move away?

Another area of inquiry involves the male partners of the natural mothers. How do they live out the natural lifestyle, and what are their reasons for doing so? This study shows men exhibiting varying levels of commitment to this type of parenting. Some supported naturalism in concrete ways, by doing the marketing, dispensing the homeopathic remedies, and tending to the organic garden. But a much larger percentage of husbands, partners, and fathers participated mainly by not creating obstacles. That is, they neither actively supported nor thwarted the mothers' agenda; in a word, their role was *passive*. For instance, the fathers agreed to share their bed with the baby, but they "could have gone either way," as one mother put it. Typically, the fathers did not resist when the mothers chose to stay at home instead of work for pay (although there were exceptions). Hearing from men directly would enhance our understanding of both natural mothering and men's response to this particular ideology and practice.

A final line of inquiry related to this topic concerns the sexual lives of natural mothers and their male partners. Does the pursuit of the natural life extend to sexual practice in some way? Sexual behavior may prove an interesting site in which to examine the paradox of natural mothering—the tension between female agency (to make change and resist norms) and compliance with gender-based roles. Who is in power in the bedroom, and how does sex figure in the ideology of natural mothering? Presumably the natural mothers regard sex as a natural, instinctual, expressive act, but what else? The bedroom is surely as important as the hearth in conceptualizing who is doing what for whom and why.

The Politics of Studying Privilege

Once the evidence became overwhelming that natural mothering was a uniquely white, middle-class enterprise, I struggled with the value of studying this privileged group of women. Many lived a life that looked difficult, certainly labor-intensive, and bereft of many of the material comforts we typically associate with class privilege. Yet the fact that they chose to live this way and could choose to live differently preserved their middle-class status. I wondered aloud, to friends and colleagues, What is the point of studying privileged white women? Do we (meaning a community of feminist knowledge-seekers) need this study? How can we use this information? Do I wish to count myself among the many who have shed light on the lives of a few who already enjoy so much public attention? What, ultimately, would be the social gain? I humbly decided that one redeeming feature of this research would be the discussion of that very privilege.

This decision did not completely resolve the matter, and my discomfort reemerged in a different, even an insidious, form. I developed a critique that at times indicted women for their choices instead of taking to task a social system that sets women up to make choices that serve the interests of men. Shouldn't I criticize the system that teaches and rewards biological determinism and gender-role-bound behaviors? Where is the critique of men who enable women's subordination? And where is the discussion of social institutions (such as public education and health care) whose inadequacy forces people to search for alternatives?

exactly

Throughout this work, I often fail to address these questions and instead criticize natural mothers for the contradictory rationales they advance to explain their lifestyle. This is a classic instance of woman blaming. Calling attention to the mothers' faults in logic, their classist blind spots, their compromised commitment to feminism, indicts them as individuals. Shouldn't we be celebrating women for making the best of their lot? The natural mothers, cleverly, it could be argued, take stock of the socially prescribed roles available to women and transform them into ones in which they feel powerful. In many ways, natural mothers are agents of their lives; they have converted the emblem of their oppression into some measure of power. As they resist convention and carve out an alternative life for themselves and their families, they redefine contemporary motherhood. Like their predecessors in female moral reform, they embrace their motherhood and use it to say something bigger—something about social values. Ultimately, they use their motherhood as a site of resistance. Where is the applause for these mothers? Where are the accolades for a group of women who are infinitely resourceful, dedicated, and clever?

As I write these questions, I remember the many people who responded to my descriptions of natural mothers with dismay and even disgust. Some readers and listeners found something distressing about a group of white women who pour the bulk of their energy into building the perfect family and virtually ignore the rest of the world. Some reacted to what they perceived as patent self-righteousness and the way the natural mothers judged other mothers who bought store-made cookies and disposable diapers. Is this classic horizontal hostility, a form of mother-to-mother competitiveness, or a genuine critique of a lifestyle that rises out of privilege, thereby exposing itself to charges of exclusivity and narrowness?

Clearly I have struggled and will continue to struggle with these questions, and I hope the reader will as well. I offer this analysis believing that we must at least have these conversations. When a pattern or trend emerges—in this case a style of mothering that promises social change—we are challenged to take a closer look and ask what, how, and, especially, who benefits?

99, 100. Bobel's tone implys disrespect for NM.
105. Resistance (NM) of mainstream culture
108 what certain NM think of mainstream institutions
111. The NM speak of the home as a refugue.
116. NM: The home, the alternative lifestyle, offers
space, to evaluate (the mainstream, etc).
This isn't about being completly free, but
a refuge.
124. NM: distrust of institutions and resentment about being
told what to do.
125. Bobel is offended by the natural mothers talk of
the 'other' mothers

126. Bobel: "NM's are not the only critics of mainstream culture... But they are distinguished by <u>their abiding faith in nature</u>

127. Bobel: "NMs speak of a pure concept of nature"... but this view denies that nature is also culturally constr and dynamic." uc

129. importance of <u>trust</u>.

131. are nms talking about superiority of men or difference to men?

133. NM: maternal self-sacrifice is <u>not</u> the problem, a culture that casts mother and child in opposition is.

133. <u>Bobel</u>: "among the serious reprocussions of the merged mother-child identity at the root of NM is the way it ~~Argan~~ marginalizes the father."

- As the primary ~~breadwinner~~ breadwinner:
- As second best caregiver to the ~~baby~~/child

137. NM: on needs of mothers (not just children) mothers have developmental stages too. when <u>both</u> are ready, we ~~can~~ can move on.

139. on what seems to be ~~loud~~ doubts by the NM can be attributed to the fact that the mainstream culture is so set up on false generalizations that it is difficult for them to break out of this veil.

144. NM: rebuilding effort - to resist mechanized motherhood. They may offer social change <u>simply</u> <u>by</u> example: social change through day to day mothering

149: NM: just "knowing"

152. Bobel tries to argue that ~~th~~ NM can only be done w/ higher-income families. I disagree w/ a lot of her points here.

153 → Bobel is using what the natural mothers say about "choice" to try to show that they have #$. But "choice", according to the NM, may mean <u>consciousness</u> not income.

·55. The NM tend to emphasise power of family over structural (#$) realities

·55 Borel presents a good question: "what's it gonna take for it to become more accessible to more people"?

Appendix

On Being a (Quasi) Natural Mother Studying Natural Mothers

In some ways I define myself as a natural mother. I gave birth at home (with the assistance of a direct-entry midwife). I nursed my (partially vaccinated) daughter until she was nearly one and a half. We eat a largely "natural foods" diet (with occasional exceptions for ice cream and store-bought cookies), and I prefer homeopathic and herbal remedies when we are ill. But unlike the natural mothers, I work full-time outside the home and do not aspire to be a full-time stay-at-home mother. Since my daughter was three months of age, she has spent at least part of every weekday in the care of someone other than myself, including paid, nonfamilial caregivers. Now eight years old, she attends public school. My deviation from the "script" of natural mothering is rooted in my resistance to subordinating my needs completely to my child's and my discomfort with essentialized conceptions of women. Furthermore, while I find some wisdom in nature, I rely on multiple sources of knowledge to shape my lifestyle and aspire to a variant of natural mothering that concerns itself with more than the individual family in its current racialized and class-based configuration. My own feminist stance leads me to find natural mothering,

175

as it is currently theorized and actualized, yet another accommodation to male privilege.

But it was the similarities between myself and the natural mothers that figured most prominently in this research process. In fact, it was my own identity as a (quasi) natural mother that led me to this particular population in the first place. A number of my friends identified as natural mothers (not in word, but in deed), and my everyday practices (shopping at the food co-op, for example) led me to interact with an even larger number of women who appeared to be natural mothers as well. Later, when I decided to study natural mothers, I relied on the common ground I had already established with the others I identified as similar to myself. This story is not unusual; many researchers mine their own lived experience for scholarly projects.

Encountering the Natural Mothers

I joined Creating Stronger Families (CSF) for two reasons: to find support for my own alternative lifestyle and to explore the possibility of studying natural mothers for my dissertation research. It is difficult to say whether my growing attachment to the group—and especially certain individuals who became friends before they were informants—or my burgeoning fascination with the topic accounts for my continued participation in CSF. I suspect it was both, each impulse feeding, shaping, and informing the other.

It would be dishonest to deny that while I was meeting personal needs, my professional agenda was always on my mind. Because I was committed to my research agenda, I interacted with each mother strategically. As I spoke with natural mothers in the context of CSF, I struck up conversations that highlighted our shared commitments to extended breastfeeding. I proudly shared my homebirth stories and my struggle with our family physician over our plan to waive the pertussis and oral polio vaccinations. In sum, I downplayed our differences but never denied them. I invested myself in building trust and cultivated my identity as a member of the "in group." And, as I explain below, after several months of community building and constructing this basis of trust, I slowly approached selected mothers and requested interviews. I first asked the ones I knew best, expecting them to feel less threatened by my research because they regarded me as a peer first and a student second. This strategy proved successful.

Both costs and benefits were associated with my insider status. Because I was a known entity, the mothers seemed to trust me, leading to more open, honest, and revealing interviews. And the combination of my own lived experience of natural mothering and the privilege of interacting personally with many of the women I interviewed prepared me to ask insightful, incisive questions. We had read many of the same books; we had encountered many of the same doubts, resistances, joys, and fears. This personal connection nurtured a level of intimacy during the interviews that often prevented the mothers from responding to questions defensively or, worse, incompletely. Occasionally, when I posed a particularly personal or controversial question, I would infuse the query with my own experience, leading with: "Something I have struggled with is . . . have you?" or: "One of the criticisms I have heard is . . ." It was often helpful to introduce a line of inquiry with a narrative of my own experience as a natural mother. In this way, I not only elicited richer responses, but I eroded my privilege as the detached, impersonal observer by inserting myself in the research process—an approach consistent with my commitment to feminist research methodology.

But there were hazards as well as benefits associated with my insider status. The most dramatic of these was the risk of "going native." Did my own identity as a natural mother and regular association with natural mothers in a variety of contexts (potlucks, conferences, private homes, parks, online communities) cost me my critical distance and therefore my analytical edge? One reader detected evidence that this was indeed the case. My writing, she noted, was sometimes too sympathetic and often romantic—not scholarly enough. I erred in taking for granted some of natural mothering's truisms. I sometimes wrote without reflection. Yet a different reader of a later draft picked up in my writing a tone of contempt for the natural mothers' choices. Had I overcompensated, or had the reader brought to the text her own biases regarding natural mothering?

Accompanying the obvious risks and benefits of my insider status during this process is a question of ethics. Throughout the data collection phase, a particular question haunted me (and at least one other reader). Did I inauthentically pose as "just another mom looking for community" when I had a research agenda in mind? My own natural mothering practices have always been authentic and freely chosen in my own and my family's best interests, and therefore it was perfectly appropriate to join CSF. But I did not immediately disclose to the membership that my reasons for joining the group were twofold and that I brought to it a researcher's lens. During the preliminary fieldwork I rationalized that my "coming out" as someone who wished to study natural mothers must be carefully timed to occur after a solid base of trust had been laid. I watched and waited until it felt safe to share my intentions. And since I was personally invested in the group's discussions and activities, and since my research agenda was one of *two* reasons for my membership, I could ethically wait to share my plans. Therefore, it was several months before I shared with members that I had chosen a dissertation topic and that my topic was the very lifestyle they practiced; few even knew that I was a student, as the assumption within the group was that all the women were full-time mothers—an assumption I did not correct until later.

I used none of the field notes I took during the potlucking and conferencing phase of this project as raw data: I could not; I did not have informed consent to do so. Rather, I used my months in the "field" to shape my questions and generally grow familiar with the population I planned to interview, so that when I did embark on the interviewing phase, I would do so with a much clearer charge.

Slowly I began speaking of my research plans, and several months into my association with the group I began approaching mothers for interviews. To my relief, as I stated earlier, most mothers were enthusiastic about the research and very willing to participate. I am quite certain that their enthusiasm was connected to their confidence that the research would be fair and well-informed, since it was being conducted by "one of our own." And I hope that they were right.

Had I shared my intentions from the start, I doubt that I would have gained access to the natural mothers as honest and forthcoming informants. In fact, I doubt that I would have been able to interview them at all, given their nearly universal distrust of scholarly research and institutionally connected "experts." Was it worth it? Let the readers, among them the very women at the center of this study, decide.

Studying Natural Mothers

> Essential meanings of women's lives can be grasped only by listening to
> the women themselves.
> —Anne Kasper, "A Feminist Qualitative Methodology" (1994, p. 266)

Because I was interested in what natural mothers themselves experienced (and thought and felt about those experiences), I undertook a qualitative study that utilized indepth, topical life-history interviews. I chose this method of data collection because I was interested in subjective accounts of the social lives of a particular contemporary population. Instead of soliciting answers to a standardized survey administered to a large group of people, I elected a more flexible and dynamic method intended to discover the informant's own "perspectives on their lives, experiences, or situations expressed in their own words" (Taylor and Bogdan, 1984, p. 77).[1]

I approached this research in much the same way the sociologist Anne Kasper designed her study of survivors of breast cancer (1994). Basing her design on the assumption that every woman is her own expert, Kasper posed open-ended questions that permitted her informants to tell their own stories. In my own study, this often meant abandoning my interview guide when it constrained talk or artificially directed the conversation. In fact, I typically opened each interview by posing one question and allowing the interview to flow from that point. Predictably, the stories I heard seldom unfolded chronologically. Rather, they were topically driven, looping back and forth to embellish, explain, or clarify where necessary.[2] Like Kasper, who argues that the nondirective approach to interviewing allows the researcher to "uncover the logic of a woman's life" (1994, p. 279), I encouraged women to point out to me the salient features of their natural mothering practice and the meanings those features had for them.[3]

Data Collection

Phase One—Finding the Natural Mothers: Initially, I looked for natural mothers in several locations: natural food stores, a local whole foods buying club, farmers' markets, La Leche League meetings, childbirth classes, homeschooling organizations (in both the unschooling and the Christian traditions), two mother support groups (one originating from a health clinic and another a spinoff from a childbirth education class), a Waldorf-inspired Saturday morning playgroup and related activities, and the local network of direct-entry midwives and their clients. Next, I immersed myself in various natural mothering communities discovered through these contacts. I joined a food buying club (where I met natural mothers monthly for food pickup and conversation), and together with my daughter I attended a Waldorf playgroup regularly for a full year. I also involved myself in the group's effort to found a Waldorf kindergarten.

Early in my preliminary fieldwork I discovered the organization that I have called Creating Stronger Families to protect the anonymity of the women I interviewed.

I became involved with CSF by attending its annual fall conference, which featured member-run workshops on topics like "Co-Housing and Other Approaches to Community," "Alternatives to Money," "Spending Less and Living More," "Alternative Energy for Our Homes," and "Finding Joy in Mothering," as well as several how-to workshops such as making cloth dolls, juggling, beginning basketry, book binding, printing, and weaving. Soon after, I joined a local subgroup whose major activity was a monthly Saturday evening potluck combined with a working bee at a member family's home (where the group toiled on various home improvements, such as building a shed) or engaged in a discussion (examples: "How We've Each Simplified the Holiday Season," "Being Different in a Mainstream Culture," and "Sharing Our Vision for Our Families"). Sometimes the (often heady) discussion or labor-intensive project was replaced by board games, group singing, or volleyball. Each potluck was announced by the host family, which selected the postdinner activity or discussion topic and sent out invitations (often hand-written). In the spirit of community and low-impact living, members were expected to bring a dish or two "to pass," their own tableware, and beverages. I attended these monthly potlucks for over a year (from winter 1995 to summer 1997), hosting two of them when my turn came up in the rotation.

In addition to my avid potlucking, I attended CSF's weekend-long winter retreat, which involved sleeping and eating in shared spaces with other families from all over the upper Midwest. Food preparation and cleanup were handled collectively. Participants engaged in workshops on homeschooling, self-sufficiency, vegetarian cooking, utopian societies, and community building, among other topics. Leisure activities included singing, dancing, hanging out in the commons area, hiking, and many children's activities. In summer 1996 I played a central role in forming a spinoff of CSF's local subgroup for families who found it difficult to travel to the nearest city. Like its parent group, the spinoff held monthly potlucks in members' homes. Throughout my association with CSF, I contributed to and received its networking directory, which lists its membership base with detailed information about each family's interests and, where applicable, services for sale or barter (many in CSF are self-employed). I also received CSF's bimonthly newsletter, which explores various topics of group interest in some depth and announces upcoming events.[4]

Although I obtained access to a good number of natural mothers through CSF, I tapped several additional networks and stayed connected with them in an attempt to expand and diversify my data base. Because I had encountered a strikingly homogeneous population at the CSF functions, Waldorf festivals, natural food stores, and holistic health and birth classes I frequented, I redoubled my efforts to recruit natural mothers who were not white, middle-class, heterosexual, married, and college-educated. To this end, I obtained access to the international network of natural mothers by subscribing to three online discussion groups (one for feminist stay-at-home mothers, one for self-defined attachment parents, and another for proponents of Jean Liedloff's continuum concept). Still, as far as I could tell, the demographic profiles were similar: The natural mothers I encountered online were largely middle-class women with at least some college education, married, and probably, although not necessarily, heterosexual. The participants talked of their husbands, their previous white-collar careers, their homes, and other resources in ways that suggested middle-class membership. I could not, of course, determine racial or ethnic identity from this electronic medium, but searching for diversity on the internet is unlikely to produce positive results, given that the majority of internet users are white males (Kehoe and Pitkow, 1996).

Still searching for diversity, I subscribed to a plethora of special-interest "alternative" magazines and newsletters (i.e., publications not available on conventional newsstands) geared to individuals seeking information about Voluntary Simplicity or Attachment Parenting. Among them were the

Compleat Mother, Welcome Home (support for stay-at-home mothers), *Homebase* (published by a Canadian organization called Mothers Are Women), *Plain* (published by the Center for Plain Living), *Simple Living Journal, Doula* (geared to birth issues), *The Nurturing Parent,* and *Informed Alternatives in Parenting.* These resources helped me understand more fully the nature and scope of the two larger trends that intersect with Cultural Feminism to create the natural mothering movement. It also affirmed the movement's class- (and possibly race-) specificity. *Mothering,* a periodical referred to by many of the mothers I spoke to and known by almost all, boasts an affluent, well-educated, mature, international readership in excess of 200,000. Specifically, the readers' median household income is $50,000; their mean age is 36 years; and 96 percent attended college (74 percent graduated, and 30 percent hold postgraduate degrees; see *Mothering,* 1994).

Although a precise demographic profile of the larger universe of natural mothers is impossible to obtain, I grew increasingly confident that lack of diversity is a key characteristic. As a result, I expanded my inquiry to address the reasons for this homogeneity.

Phase Two— Interviewing: I first approached a small number of the mothers with whom I had become familiar as a result of my association with CSF. Believing the natural mothering population to be highly research-skeptical, I had decided earlier not to request permission to collect participant-observation data during the first phase of the project. I had heard many remarks about insensitive and unenlightened institutions (such as colleges and universities) and exploitative, self-important, so-called experts (like academic researchers), and feared that my own requests for interviews would be denied. Two events reinforced my impression of a research-resistant population.

Shortly before I began approaching women for interviews, an article entitled "Does Research Help Families Interested in Alternatives?" appeared in CSF's newsletter. Its author, a mother and one of the founders of the organization, raised several points for people to consider when asked to participate in studies of "alternative living"—which reportedly was happening with increasing frequency. Among them were: "Does research dehumanize the people it uses as subjects?" "Does the process of participating in a study undermine people's confidence?" Around the same time, a psychologist and CSF member (but not a regular participant in group functions) sent a mass mailing to the organization's membership announcing her intention to begin calling families and requesting their participation in an experimental study of the parent–child attachment process. Several recipients complained about the invasion of privacy, and the coordinator of CSF directed the psychologist to send out a retraction and an apology. She was forced to look elsewhere for participants, and I was left feeling that I might encounter a similar reaction to my interview requests.

Luckily, my early fieldwork not only protected me from a similar fate but assisted me in designing a stronger study. The interviews I ultimately conducted and used as data were legitimated by my prior role as a participant. In addition, the months I spent getting to know various natural mothers while immersed in the loosely structured community of like-minded women shaped the interviews' format and content. My preliminary fieldwork and "insider" status also made me a "known entity" among the natural mothers, facilitating referrals to other potential informants.

To my great relief, when I finally did approach women to request interviews, all but two agreed. I wondered if their willingness to participate was a reflection of the trust I had worked to foster or my own misinterpretation of their opinion of academic research. The former explanation seems more appropriate, since the interviews I later conducted confirmed that natural mothers are indeed generally put off by scholars and others associated with institutions of higher learning.

Two women declined to be interviewed. One woman's denial was especially unfortunate because many regarded her as a role model. She and her husband had co-founded CSF, and she was also the author of "Does Research Help Families Interested in Alternatives?" When I first contacted her, she requested "some time to think about it." We agreed that I would call again in two weeks. When I called as scheduled, she politely but assertively declined my interview request for two reasons: (1) Her life was too busy then ("Not very Simple Living, huh?" she quipped), and (2) she was "not comfortable participating in [any, she implied] research," but could not "really explain why." Intrigued by her refusal, I pressed her for specific reasons, expecting a summary of the arguments she had made in the CSF newsletter, but she could not or would not provide them. Perhaps I, as a relative insider, posed less of a threat to her than the unknown inquisitor she imagined when she wrote her article, so she was at a loss to explain why she was unwilling to cooperate with someone known to her with apparently honorable intentions. Another woman took three days to respond to my request and then e-mailed me explaining that she was just "too busy."

To determine whether a referral was appropriate to my study, I created a rather loose set of criteria. The major criterion was simply that informants must be committed to the principles of Voluntary Simplicity and Attachment Parenting to some degree. In addition, informants must engage in at least one of the following practices: (1) homeschooling, (2) extended breastfeeding (beyond the first year), (3) home birth, (4) alternative medicine (homeopathy, herbalism, naturopathy, etc.), and(5) the consumption of a diet derived largely from whole or natural foods. I intentionally omitted any reference to political or religious orientation as I suspect that there is a great deal of variability along those dimensions and I wished to capture as much of it as possible.

All but one interview was conducted in the informant's home (one woman suggested that she come to my house because her husband was home with their four young children, and she anticipated a more productive interview with no children present). Children were in fact present for most interviews, playing at our feet or in a nearby room. When I requested interviews, most women asked if children could be present. I learned after the first few conversations that the mothers' participation depended on the presence of their children. These women rarely use babysitters for any reason, least of all to accommodate a researcher. Interviews lasted between one and one-half and three hours, with the majority filling two hours. Many interviews were interrupted by childcare responsibilities, which cut into talk time but reaffirmed my understanding of natural mothers as women who put the everyday harmony of the house and what they define as their children's needs before everything else.

The interviews were very loosely structured, although I kept a detailed list of questions nearby and committed to memory. I typically opened interviews with a simple question: "How did you get to this place as a mom who practices alternatives in her family life?" Interested in what the mothers considered most central to their decision(s) to "live differently," I intentionally gave no further direction (on a few occasions, I suggested a number of common access points I had heard repeatedly, but I resorted to this guidance only when a mother genuinely seemed stumped).

As anticipated, women began their tales at a variety of places. Some responded to this open-ended query: "Well, I guess I will start with my childhood . . ." while others traced their steps beginning with their decision to become a vegetarian or nurse their first-born. Still others initially remembered reading a "life-changing" book (as one woman phrased it) like *The Continuum Concept* by Jean Liedloff (1985) or La Leche League International's *Womanly Art of Breastfeeding* (1958, first edition).

In the spring of 1996, I interviewed four women to clarify the direction of the research and hone my interviewing skills. The following year (winter/spring 1997), I interviewed the remaining women. I ultimately contacted 43 women and completed 32 interviews. Of the 11 women contacted but not interviewed, nine were willing to participate but found it impossible to schedule an interview for one reason or another, and two scheduled interviews but canceled at the last moment because their children were ill.

I chose to interview a relatively small number of women for two reasons. First, I wanted to analyze my data closely in a way that a larger sample would make difficult. Second, as I neared my thirtieth interview, I hit a saturation point, indicated by a decreasing number of new ideas and conceptual themes turning up in the interviews. The data collection reached a point where I was able to anticipate what informants would say before they uttered the words. The strategy of "theoretical sampling" is relevant here (Glaser and Strauss, 1967). In theoretical sampling, the number of "cases" studied (in this case, the number of women interviewed) is less important than the quality of data derived from each research encounter. In other words, the researcher is concerned with "developing theoretical insights into the area of social life being studied" (Taylor and Bogdan, 1984, p. 83). Accordingly, once I had completed several interviews, I began seeking negative evidence for emerging hypotheses in subsequent interviews. I also sought to arrange interviews with women who were single, nonwhite, poor, and lesbian, and was successful in finding a few mothers who satisfied some of these requirements.[5]

During the first four interviews, I asked for referrals and thus initiated a snowball sampling procedure. Although I had met a sufficient number of potential informants in my preinterview work, I wanted to capture as diverse a sample as possible. The snowball sampling method of collecting informants is quite effective in reaching hard-to-access populations, like the research-skeptical natural mothers. Yet it presents the problem of external validity. Because I drew informants mostly from a specific region in the Midwest, it is likely that my informant pool is uniquely Midwestern in character, demonstrating regional specificity.

Moreover, if we assume that people select others as friends on the basis of shared characteristics, then relying on snowball sampling may well have created an interview pool of women similar along a number of dimensions beyond their commitment to natural mothering (such as race and class).[6] Because it is impossible to enumerate the larger universe of natural mothers, I cannot know how representative my particular sample is (although I have some ideas, as described earlier). Therefore, I cannot generalize from my study to the universe of natural mothers. Instead, this qualitative investigation seeks to provide an in-depth understanding through a close analysis of a small sample. It is my hope that the study's data-grounded interpretations will serve as springboards for subsequent studies.

The in-depth interviewing method "enables us to know people intimately, to see the world through their eyes, and to enter into their experiences vicariously" (Taylor and Bogdan, 1984, citing Shaw, 1931), but it simultaneously raises questions of internal validity. Because interviews rely on individuals' best recollections of life events, there is always the possibility that the information shared is less than accurate. Embellishments, exaggerations, deceptions, and distortions all potentially affect the quality of the data, and as a researcher I have no foolproof means of separating fact from fiction.

However, my many months of preliminary fieldwork (which continued during the interviewing phase) proved quite useful in reducing this type of error. I was able to observe natural mothers living out some of the beliefs they described to me (such as breastfeeding an older child in public, cooking and serving whole foods, or using a bicycle as a primary form of transportation). My participant- observation provided the setting and the opportunity to confirm the veracity of informants' words. Therefore, I am confident that most of the information relayed to me was as accurate and reliable as one could expect.

Protecting Informants—Ethical Concerns: To protect the anonymity of the women I interviewed, I used pseudonyms for them and others mentioned in the interviews. Information that could point to someone's true identity was altered in a way that best reflected the facts without jeopardizing her privacy. The master list of informants' full names and consent forms have been stored separately from the original tapes and one set of backup copies (which typically refer to informants only by their first names).

A Demographic Profile of the Sample: I did my best to eschew standard experimental conventions that highlight the distinction between observer and observed. Generally, I attempted to create a research environment that more closely simulated a conversation between acquaintances. More specifically, I chose not to administer a survey for the purposes of collecting demographic data; instead, I combed the interview transcripts for such information. This information is summarized in Table 1, suggesting the range of the sample along a variety of dimensions.

The 32 women I interviewed ranged in age from 29 to 56, with a mean age of 37. All were white, and apparently heterosexual. Most reported growing up in middle-class families, although a few were raised poor and a few were raised in wealthier homes.[7]

Eighty-eight percent of informants were married (14 percent of the married women were remarried). The range of years married was five through 33. Two women had never been married but were involved in committed partnerships at the time of their children's conception, birth, and early years. One woman was newly separated and planning a divorce; another had been divorced for several years.

The women averaged 2.6 children each. Ten women had four children, four had three, 14 had two, and four had one child. These figures include three expected children (three women were pregnant at the time of the interviews) and three stepchildren. The children ranged from infancy to 28 years. All the women breastfed at least one child, although not all children were breastfed (interestingly, once one child was breastfed, all the subsequent children were as well). Breastfeeding duration varied from five weeks to almost five years. The mean age of weaning was three years. Nationally, 59.7 percent of mothers initiate breastfeeding, and 21 percent of those mothers are still breastfeeding at six months (Ryan, 1997). Ruth Lawrence (1996) estimates that

Table 1. Demographic Characteristics of Natural Mothers

Education level	
Attended college	81%
High school diploma	13
Some college	13
Four-year college degree	47
Postgraduate	22
No information	5
Age	
20–29	9
30–39	41
40–49	41
50–59	9
Sexual orientation	
Heterosexual	100
Racial/ethnic background	
White/Caucasian	100
Marital status	
Married	88
Single, never married	6
Separated	3
Divorced	3
Children	
1	12
2	44
3	12
4	32
Breastfeeding duration (in years)	
1	9
2	9
3	19
3.5	16
4	9
5	3
Not specified	37
Homeschooling (at any time)	62

Table I. *Continued*

Residential status	
Own own home	87%
Urban	31
Small town	46
Rural	23
Paid labor status	
Full-time employment	3
Part-time employment	34
Previous career	50
Husband's job	
White-collar profession	62
Self-employed (at some time)	36
Vegetarian lifestyle	36
Family bed	62
Affiliated with La Leche League	65
International travel	
Lived abroad	34
Traveled extensively	19
Home birth	32
Own a television	50
Own a computer	33

the worldwide age of weaning is 2.8 years, while Katherine Detwyler (1997) estimates a range of five to seven years.[8]

At least 81 percent of the women I interviewed had at least attended college. The specific breakdown is as follows:

No college = 4
Attended college but did not graduate = 4
Earned bachelor's degree = 15
Attended graduate school but did not finish = 2

Master's degree = 3
Ph.D. = 2
No information = 2

Work experiences outside the home varied widely. Exactly one-half had formerly engaged in careers, which I defined as having a coherent and upwardly mobile professional or semiprofessional work history. Three of the women were nurses, and three were teachers. One woman was a social worker, another a college librarian and adjunct instructor, another a research ecologist, and another a physical therapist. There was a mechanical artist, an engineer, a music transcriptionist, a coordinator of state-funded daycare programs, and a political organizer whose work centered on environmental and labor issues. This list is not exhaustive but conveys the range of careers held by the women interviewed.

At the time of the interviews, only one woman held a full-time job (she was one of the two single mothers in the sample). Several women (34 percent) worked part-time, "keeping their hand in their careers" or "pulling in a little extra money." Of these employed women, most worked out of their homes and were thus able to be at home full-time with their children and maintain their identity as stay-at-home mothers.

The women's husbands worked in a variety of occupations, including software engineer, social worker, physician (in fact, four of the husbands were physicians), janitor, carpenter, physical therapist, assistant school superintendent, musician, and college instructor. About two-thirds worked in white-collar professions. Of all the husbands, regardless of type of career or job, 36 percent had been self-employed at some time in their adult work history.

Religious affiliation varied. Among the sample were one Jew, three "born again" Christians, one Mennonite, six

Catholics, one Methodist, two women who subscribed to "new age" spirituality, two nonspecific Protestants, and 16 unspecified.

Thirty-six percent of the women were vegetarians, 62 percent practiced family bed, and at least 65 percent (but I suspect more) stated that they were members of La Leche League. All but three were sympathetic to the broad aims of the feminist agenda; 44 percent identified themselves as feminists.

Thirty-two percent of the women chose to give birth to at least one child at home—the national average is 1 percent (O'Connor, 1993). Of the 62 births experienced by the total sample, 21 percent involved cesarean sections. Nationally, nearly 25 percent of deliveries are cesarean (Gabay and Wolf, 1994). Thirty-four percent of the women had lived abroad, and an additional 19 percent had traveled extensively, meaning that over half of the sample had significant cross-cultural or international exposure.

I did not collect precise information regarding the level of technological utilization (especially the presence of televisions and computers), but over half had a television (two of the families use it only for video viewing). At least one-third of the families had a computer in their home.

Many books and periodicals were mentioned during the interviews. Most notably, the periodical *Mothering* was mentioned eight times by different informants, the book *Sequencing* (1986) by Arlene Rossen Cardozo six times, *The Continuum Concept* (1985) by Jean Liedloff five times, and works by John Holt, author of several books on unschooling, six times.

Sixty-two percent of the women either had homeschooled or were currently homeschooling their children. In my sample of homeschooling families, the mothers assumed almost exclusive responsibility for their children's education. Nationally, estimates of the number of homeschooled children vary.

Patricia Lines (1991) estimates that 375,000 American children were homeschooled in the early 1990s, while B. D. Ray (1996), using different methods, calculates that one million were. Interestingly, 85 percent of parents surveyed by the National Home Education Research Institute cited religious views as the chief motivating factor in their decision to homeschool (Heckler-Feltz, 1997). Among the women I interviewed, only 15 percent identified religion as a motive.

Eighty-seven percent of the couples owned their own homes; the rest rented apartments. Forty-six percent of the women lived in small towns; 23 percent lived in rural areas; and 31 percent lived in urban areas.

Data Analysis

Like Marjorie DeVault, who studied the social organization of women's work in "feeding the family," I attempted to "use informants' words to capture fleeting realities and hold them still for close attention" (1991, p. 229). This methodological approach reflects Dorothy Smith's (1987) prescriptions for building a sociology for women that begins with an analysis of women's actual lived experience and how it is shaped by larger social relations.

Once I had collected the data, interviews were transcribed into verbatim narratives. These transcripts were then coded using a process called "open coding," which fractures the data, permitting the researcher to identify categories, including their key dimensions and descriptive properties (Strauss and Corbin, 1990). While I listened to the stories that flowed during these interviews, I was mindful of a theoretical method called "bracketing," an ethnomethodological approach that seeks to put aside taken-for-granted "truths" and understandings. Susan Kessler and Wendy

McKenna explain bracketing as a method (inspired by Husserl [1931] and other phenomenologists) that "sets aside" the "natural attitude." When we bracket or temporarily suspend our beliefs, we dissolve the "constancy and independent existence of objects, and we are left only with particular, concrete situations" (1978, p. 5). I needed bracketing to prevent my own "knowledge" from clouding my ability to grasp the content and form of the knowledge that structures and gives meaning to my informants' lives.

Once the open-coding phase was complete, I began a process known as "axial coding," defined by Anselm Strauss and Juliet Corbin as "a set of procedures whereby data are put back together in new ways ... by making connections between categories" (1990, p. 6). During this process, the researcher specifies the context (the specific set of properties) in which individual categories are situated, the action/interactional strategies associated with an individual category, and the consequences of those strategies. Ultimately, all the names and specified categories are linked to construct an overarching, comprehensive theoretical formulation. This analytical process endeavors to reveal and understand the salient issues associated with the natural mothering movement.

My interpretation is legitimated through the heavy use of verbatim quotations from the transcripts. I draw on my informants' words to construct a "thick description" on which to base my analysis, while also permitting the reader to draw her or his own conclusions as well.

The Role of Feminist Commitment in the Research Process

As a feminist, I am committed to ideas and efforts that empower women to assert their rights in society. It was this commitment that attracted me to the politically charged reality of natural mothering. Natural mothering represents a paradox—a lifestyle simultaneously progressive and regressive. For me, as a feminist and a mother, natural mothering presented an ideal topic: fraught with tangled contradictions, complicated layers of meaning, and the immediacy of a contemporary phenomenon growing rapidly but, until now, unstudied.

My feminism led me right to the voices of the women at the center of natural mothering. As a feminist who respects a woman's right to self-expression and the telling of her own stories, it made sense to ask natural mothers *themselves* what they felt about their lives and minimize, as much as possible, any authority attached to my position as academic researcher. To this end, I designed a study that relied as little as possible on my power. By providing little direction during the interviews, for example, I acknowledged that the real experts on this topic are the natural mothers.

The feminist interpretative lens may well have heightened my sensitivity to issues of inequity, power dynamics, and the social construction of gender. It compelled me to ask: What about women's power? Of course, the choice to view the world through any particular lens is also a choice *not* to view the world through another lens, and therein lie problems of bias. Yet, as a qualitative methodologist, I retain no illusions regarding the presentation of a wholly objective study through the detachment of self from scholarship. Certainly this study is subjectively conceived and executed, like all others. Nevertheless, it is my hope that the voices of 32 women speak clearly throughout these pages, enhanced with an analysis that looks critically at the more subtle dimensions embedded in their accounts.

Notes

1. Fascinated by the radicalism of the mothers I was studying, I originally used the term "radical mother" to describe them. But when I asked my informants how they felt about the label, many of them were uncomfortable with it: It "makes us sound so militant, so strident," one remarked. "Natural mothers" is consistent with the enduring respect for and trust in nature that guides their practice.

2. According to La Leche League, nipple confusion sometimes occurs in babies who are fed by both breast and bottle in the first few weeks of life. Sucking from an artificial nipple requires less work, and babies fed both ways may suck less efficiently at the breast, impeding healthy weight gain or stopping the production of mother's milk altogether (La Leche League, 1987, p. 157).

3. Family bed, alternatively known as co-sleeping and sharing sleep, is the practice of children and parents regularly sleeping together until the children express interest in sleeping in their own bed. In many cases the family acquires a king-size bed or lashes together two smaller beds to create enough sleeping area to accommodate everyone. Typically, infants and nursing toddlers occupy the family bed with Mom and Dad as a means of facilitating night-time breastfeeding, but older children are always welcome. Proponents of family bed claim that they are able to get their needed sleep only because their children are nearby at night. With family bed, Mom simply rolls over and offers the breast to the hungry or fussy child; often, she can go back to sleep soon thereafter. (Sexual activity is usually experienced elsewhere.) In my study, it was not uncommon for fathers to be less committed to the idea of family bed (after all, the practice has more obvious benefits for the nursing mother). Fathers who tire of little feet in their faces and ever-diminishing sleep space sometimes move to a spare room, the couch, an older child's bed, or a younger child's bed that is (implicitly) set up for Dad while the child is still sharing the family bed. The dads I informally spoke with seldom complained about their sleeping arrangements. Usually, they laughed or shrugged and said, "That's how it is for now." For more information on the global his-

tory and contemporary practice of family bed, see Thevenin's *The Family Bed* (1976).

4. The American Academy of Husband-Coached Childbirth teaches a method of childbirth conceived by Dr. Robert Bradley. A consumer-oriented natural approach to birth, it emphasizes deep relaxation, husbands and partners as coaches, and little or no medical intervention. Many of the natural mothers used the Bradley method to birth one or more of their children (often at home); nearly all the women I spoke with were familiar with it.

Chapter Two

1. This historical overview draws heavily on Ginsberg's study of the abortion debate (1989).

2. Childcare manuals of the Puritan period were addressed to fathers, not mothers (see Thurer, 1994).

3. Members of the "cult of true womanhood" in the nineteenth century occupied virtually the same social class position enjoyed by the natural mothers in this study. Some historical continuity appears to thread together women who can afford to attach significance to femininity, domesticity, and motherhood. Chapter 6 discusses in depth the link between class status and social change as it applies to the project of natural mothering.

4. Women who were not content may have registered their protests in covert ways; see Epstein, 1981, especially p. 86, for an interesting discussion of the Victorian "epidemic" of hysteria as women's protest.

5. In 1839 the FMRS listed 445 local auxiliaries, located primarily in New York State and New England (Smith-Rosenberg, 1979).

6. This idea was first articulated by the sociologist Lester Ward in the 1880s, but Addams popularized it through her work and writing (see Ginsberg, 1989).

7. For a fuller discussion of the women's club movement, see G. G. McBride's *On Wisconsin Women* (1994).

8. The benefits to individual reform-minded women are questionable. Shari Thurer argues that the "upgraded job description of the professional activist more likely served not to advance the status of women but to provide females with a calling in which they could excel without being threatening to males" (1994, p. 234).

9. Kathryn Kish Sklar (1993) lists a number of historical factors derived from the political culture of middle-class women and political culture in general that enabled more privileged women to provide the kind of support that working-class women could not offer each other.

10. Dual labor market theory holds that labor markets are systematically divided into a primary sector, comprising relatively high-wage jobs with advancement potential, and a secondary sector of low-pay, "dead end" jobs (Jary and Jary, 1991, p. 131). Typically, women have enjoyed less access to primary-sector jobs than their male counterparts (see Reskin and Padavic, 1994).

11. Koven and Michel suggest that maternalist politics were most effective in the weakest, least bureaucratic states, like Germany and France, and least effective in stronger states, like the United States and Britain (cited in Skocpol, 1992, p. 36). But Theda Skocpol (1992) regards the weak–strong distinction as too crude because it fails to account for the variability within individual nations' systems of government.

12. May points to the shortsightedness of the view that the demographic boom in the 1950s and 1960s was little more than "the last gasp of time-honored family life before the sixties generation made a major break from the past." In fact, "in many ways the youths of the sixties resembled their grandparents, who came of age in the first decades of the twentieth century" (1988, p. 9).

13. This rallying cry benefited middle-class women but did little for poor ones, since it is unlikely that men were perceived as potential domestic employees and childcare workers.

Chapter Three

1. A contemporary embodiment of this ideology is Coop America. For a nominal annual membership fee, members receive the organization's *Financial Planning Handbook* (a guide to socially responsible investing) and the *National Green Pages*, which advertises "green" products and services and provides periodic boycott updates (Coop America, 1998).

2. When "economic hardship" is cited as a motive for Voluntary Simplicity, one wonders how voluntary the practice actually is. Could the invocation of VS be simply a veiled attempt at after-the-fact rationalization, portraying a lifestyle necessitated by economic conditions as one chosen freely?

3. Certainly, the generalizability of Liedloff's findings is a matter for debate. She assumes that a parenting practice she observed in one culture is the most "natural" and universal because it has withstood the test of time. This view—"older equals better" because "older equals more natural"—is woven throughout the discourse of natural mothering.

4. In the interest of space, I have resisted the urge to list the exploding number of resources, including products, websites, books, and periodicals that promote individual facets of natural living, such as the acquisition and

preparation of whole, natural foods, alternative health care, organic gardening, homeschooling, and natural childbirth.

5. Because I chose to guide the flow of the early interviews as little as possible, the topic of feminism "came up" in some interviews and not in others. Later, when the importance of this theme to natural mothering became apparent, I initiated the topic, asking mothers to share their impressions of feminism and state whether or not they identified with the movement.

Chapter Four

1. Many feminists dispute the characterization of feminism as anti-motherhood. Laurie Umansky's *Motherhood Reconceived: Feminism and the Legacies of the Sixties* (1996) challenges the notion that radical and socialist feminist movements in the United States ignored or maligned the institution of motherhood. She examines books, periodical literature, and widely distributed political tracts to show a persistent feminist concern with motherhood as both a utopian frontier for countercultural ideals and the metaphorical cement needed to bind a fragmented movement together.

2. The natural mothers' portrayal of their "old feminism" (liberal) and their "new feminism" (cultural) suggests an artificial dichotomy that obscures the reality that any two feminist ideologies will not only diverge but also converge at many levels and over time.

3. In *The Way We Never Were* (1992), Stephanie Coontz convincingly explodes the myth of the typical 1950s home as composed of bread-winning father and homemaking mother. Still, this myth, I think it is safe to say, dominates the consciousness of most Americans and sets up the comparison at the root of the natural mothers' conception of mothers then and now.

4. Certainly their choices involved a series of compromises, negotiations, doing things, and undoing them better represented by a spiral than by a line. At the same time, the natural mothers' discourse evaded this complicated choice-making spiral. Many spoke of an epiphany—a moment when their choice was clear and they passed a point of no return. This oversimplified representation of choice as clean, clear, and indisputable permits the natural mothers to minimize their ambivalence about the implications of their lifestyle.

5. Several mothers spoke of rifts in familial and other relationships caused, in their estimation, by fundamental differences in parenting philosophies and practices. Jenny, for example, discussed a falling out with a former college roommate and very close friend because the friend

insisted that she needed to work outside the home and Jenny believed that she was ultimately selfish for doing so. Other women spoke of the silences they endured at family gatherings and social events when it was clear that they had little in common with the other people there. Some women shared coping strategies. Janet Mitford explained that she typically took inventory of a friend's home in order to rule out potentially contentious topics and "keep the peace." While scanning a room for items such as bottles, disposable diapers, cribs, and processed food, she would mutter to herself, "Well . . . can't talk about that. . . . Guess I won't bring that one up . . . "

6. Two hormones are released in the process of breastfeeding: prolactin and oxytocin. Prolactin is secreted to prepare a mother's breasts for milk production. Oxytocin causes muscle contraction, and because it flows more readily when a mother is feeling positive and peaceful, it has been called the "happiness hormone" and the "hormone of love" (Kitzinger, 1992).

7. This discussion may seem to contradict the earlier discussion of resisting the status quo as central to natural mothering practice, but it does not. In this context "the status quo" and "the way things have always been" refer to a historical division of parenting labor based on gender. As natural mothers defend their unconventional parenting choices, they often reclaim age-old practices such as sleeping with babies to protect them from animals (Thevenin, 1976) and carrying babies in slings to free arms and hands for work in the field and cottage industries. The "status quo" in this discussion, then, does not refer to the current, dominant way of doing things, but to a historical tradition that challenges contemporary, conventional know how.

8. "Waldorf schools" follow the schooling tradition founded by Rudolf Steiner in Germany over 70 years ago. "Anthroposophy" is the theoretical basis of Waldorf education, which eschews technological advances in the classroom and home (such as the use of television and computers) and advocates the use of toys and tools derived from natural materials like wool, silk, and wood. The arts, oral storytelling, and a dancelike form of movement called eurythmy are central to the curriculum. Steiner College, which trains teachers for Waldorf schools, states that they represent "the largest and fastest growing non-sectarian educational movement in the world"; there are currently over 500 Waldorf schools internationally (Steiner College website, *www.steinercollege.org*).

9. "Direct-entry midwife" is a descriptive label used to differentiate midwives who have completed their training through apprenticeships from certified nurse midwives (CNMs), who are nursing school graduates equipped with state licenses and hospital privileges. "Direct-entry" refers

to the midwife's immediate insertion into the field of midwifery as a practitioner-in-training (with varying levels of involvement as her skills increase). CNMs typically attend hospital births, while direct-entry midwives attend homebirths exclusively. In many states, direct-entry midwives practice midwifery illegally or with ambiguous legal standing; in Washington, Texas, and some other states, they are licensed. For a more thorough discussion of contemporary midwifery, see Sullivan and Weitz, 1988.

10. The heart symbol is common to the culture of La Leche League. I have seen more than one letter signed by League leaders with the words, "LLLove,———." While attending a regional League conference in 1996, I was struck by the ubiquitousness of hearts on League pamphlets and workshop handouts. The conference theme was "La Leche League: Heart to Heart."

11. For instance, Maria Mies (1988) challenges the long-held contention that men earn most of the family "bread." Women, she argues, produce most of the food worldwide, while men's undependable and episodic success at procuring food through hunting is surrounded by attention-getting rituals and celebrations.

Chapter Five

1. In the discourse of natural mothering, "institutions" refers to formal organizations (established, ubiquitous, socially recognized sources of authority) such as schools, hospitals and other systems of health care provision, and mental agencies. Generally speaking, natural mothers see "institutions" as the vehicles of mainstream lifestyles.

2. Fibromyalgia, a common and disabling disorder affecting 2–4 percent of the U.S. population, causes body aches, sleep disturbance, stiffness, and extreme fatigue. It is closely related to chronic fatigue syndrome (Nye, 1995).

3. Community supported agriculture (CSA) makes locally grown produce available to subscribers. For a fee, the farm delivers a share of its weekly harvest (whatever it might be that week) to the subscriber group. CSAs ensure a regular and reliable outlet for farm products while providing consumers with wholesome foods grown locally.

4. Founded by a family to promote and support a simple, family-centered lifestyle, CSF hosts retreats, an annual fall conference, and other local events to provide information and support to families who pursue alternatives such as homeschooling, home birth, extended breastfeeding, organic gardening, and the consumption of whole or "natural" foods.

5. Regrettably, I did not explore in more depth the "bargaining for baby" theme that surfaced more than once in these interviews. At this point, I can only advance a few explanations for why natural mothers in this study found themselves in the position of persuading, perhaps even coercing, their partners to expand their families. Knowing how central maternity is to the women's identities, it is not surprising that, in their view, "more is better." Moreover, while the mother is home providing full-time, intensive care and deriving meaning from doing so, the father is away, deriving his identity from paid work and nonfamilial relationships. Given this rigid division of spheres, it is not unlikely that mother and father would have different views about whether or not to have more children. Clearly, children function differently in their lives. If the main source of power for natural mothers resides in completely dependent babies, it may be necessary to replace older children with younger ones. Without babies who need her (and only her), she risks losing power.

6. On the one hand, given the conflicted relationship most natural mothers have with technology in general, it is not surprising that they cite television as the source of familial problems. However, targeting the TV as problematic is certainly not limited to natural mothers. In 1996, 49 percent of Americans reported they watched "too much TV" (TV-Free America, 1998, citing *Harpers*, 1996).

Chapter Seven

1. For instance, 23 (out of a possible 36) was the average ACT score for a homeschooler in 1998. Conventionally schooled children averaged a 21 (Kantrowitz and Wingert, 1998).

Appendix

1. "Informant" is intentionally used throughout this book. I avoid "subject" and "respondent" as I believe they connote a disengaged, even passive, participant in a research study. The word "informant" more accurately reflects the way the women I interviewed shaped the content and process of this investigation.

2. The form of the stories, consistent with feminist understandings of women's narrative style, was perhaps more a web than a straight line (Langellier and Peterson, 1984).

3. The life-history method, also known as sociological autobiography, is rooted in the rich tradition of the Chicago School of urban ethnography. Beginning in the 1920s and throughout the 1940s, Robert Park, W. I. Thomas, Ernest Burgess, and later Everett C. Hughes and his student

Howard Becker departed from the more conventional survey approach and developed Chicago-style sociology (see Van Maanen, 1988). Perhaps the greatest legacy of the ethnographic tradition in social science research is that it allows research questions to be guided by the informants rather than arbitrarily determined by the researcher.

4. I wish to clarify that this book is *not* an investigation of CSF. While a substantial number of my informants were drawn from this organization, the interviews focused on individual women's experience of natural mothering, not their experience of membership in the organization per se. An organizational study of CSF would, however, prove very valuable, as it would surely illuminate how grassroots organizations shape larger social movements.

5. The following story indicated the almost universal "whiteness" of the natural mothering population I encountered: When I inquired about women of color who might be appropriate for my study, two responses were typically given. Either the informant admitted that she knew no women of color who "fit the description" of a natural mother, or she provided the name of an African American regional coordinator of La Leche League, the *only* woman of color whose name I ever received. Unfortunately, I was unable to interview her.

6. Rosabeth Moss Kanter's notion of homosocial reproduction may be relevant here (1977, pp. 54, 63). Kanter argues that employers hire the applicants who most resemble themselves, thereby reproducing a homogeneous work force in certain niches. The same dynamic is most likely in operation when snowball sampling is utilized.

7. The designations "middle-class," "poor," and "wealthier" are derived from the language of the informants themselves. I did not collect income information to check the accuracy of these labels. What was important to me was not an individual's true class affiliation, but rather her class-based *identity*.

8. The assertion "Well, you know, the world-wide age of weaning is 4.2 years" has been used to justify long-term nursing by La Leche League leaders and members and others who support extended breastfeeding. I heard it repeatedly in my interactions with natural mothers. The statistic originated with Ruth Lawrence (1994, p. 312). Yet Lawrence provides no documentation for this figure, attributing it to a Ross Labs brochure that, according to Ross Labs, is no longer available (K. Detwyler, personal communication, June 17, 1998). See Detwyler (1997) for a discussion of the impossibility of defining a world-wide age of weaning, given the importance of cultural context in initiating and supporting breastfeeding. For a provocative discussion of the "nursing debate" (featuring a nursing mother of four-year-old twin girls), see Sara Corbett's "The Breast Offense" (2001).

References

Alster, Kristin (1989). *The Holistic Health Movement*. Tuscaloosa: University of Alabama Press.

Andrews, Cecile. *The Circle of Simplicity: Return to the Good Life*. New York: HarperCollins, 1997.

Arms, Suzanne (1975). *Immaculate Deception: A New Look at Women and Childbirth in America*. Boston: Houghton Mifflin.

Baldwin, Rahima (1979). *Special Delivery*. Millbrae, Calif.: Les Femmes.

Bartky, Sandra Lee (1990). *Femininity and Domination: Studies in the Phenomenology of Oppression*. New York: Routledge.

Belenky, Mary, et al. (1986). *Women's Ways of Knowing: The Development of Self, Voice and Mind*. New York: Basic Books.

Bem, Sandra (1974). "The Measurement of Psychological Androgyny." *Journal of Consulting and Clinical Psychology*, 42, 155–62.

Bender, Sue (1989). *Plain and Simple: A Woman's Journey to the Amish*. New York: Harper.

Berger, Peter, and Luckmann, Thomas (1967). *The Social Construction of Reality: A Treatise in the Sociology of Knowledge*. Garden City, N.Y.: Anchor Books.

Blum, Linda, and Vandewater, Elizabeth (1993). " 'Mother to Mother': A Maternalist Organization in Late Capitalist America." *Social Problems*, 40, 285–300.

Bobel, Chris (2001). "Bounded Liberation: A Focused Study of La Leche League." *Gender and Society*, 15, 131–52.

Boggs, Carl (1986). *Social Movements and Political Power: Emerging Forms of Radicalism in the West*. Philadelphia: Temple University Press.

Borchert, James (1982). *Alley Life in Washington: Family, Community, Religion and Folklife in the City, 1850–1970*. Urbana: University of Illinois Press.

Brophy, Beth (1995). "Stressless—and Simple—in Seattle." *U.S. News & World Report*, December 11, p. 96.

Buechler, Steven (2000). *Social Movements in Advanced Capitalism*. New York: Oxford University Press.

Cardozo, Arlene Rossen (1986). *Sequencing: Having It All but Not All at Once*. New York: Atheneum.

Celente, Gerald (1997). *Trends 2000: How to Prepare for and Profit from the Changes of the Twentieth Century*. New York: Warner Books.

Chodorow, Nancy (1978). *The Reproduction of Mothering: Psychoanalysis and the Sociology of Gender*. Berkeley: University of California Press.

Cohen, Jean (1985). "Strategy or Identity: New Theoretical Paradigms and Contemporary Social Movements." *Social Research*, 52, 663–717.

Connell, R. W. (1987). *Gender and Power*. Stanford, Calif.: Stanford University Press.

Coontz, Stephanie (1993). *The Way We Never Were: American Families and the Nostalgia Trap*. New York: Basic Books.

Coop America (1998). Membership Information (brochure). Washington, D.C.: Author.

Corbett, Sara (2001). "The Breast Offense." *New York Times Magazine*, May 6, pp. 82–85.

Cott, Nancy (1977). *The Bonds of Womanhood: "Woman's Sphere" in New England 1780–1835*. New Haven: Yale University Press.

Cronon, William (ed.) (1995). *Uncommon Ground: Toward Reinventing Nature*. New York: W. W. Norton.

Dacycyzn, Amy (1993). *The Tightwad Gazette: Promoting Thrift as a Viable Alternative Lifestyle*. New York: Random House.

——— (1999). *The Complete Tightwad Gazette: Promoting Thrift as a Viable Alternative Lifestyle*. New York: Random House.

de Graaf, John, and Boe, Vivia (producers) (1997). *Affluenza* (film). Available from Bullfrog Films, P.O. Box 149, Oley, Pa. 19457.

Detwyler, Kathryn (1997). "Breastfeeding, Weaning and Other Infant and Child Feeding Issues: A Research Guide for Field and Clinic." Manuscript.

DeVault, Marjorie (1991). *Feeding the Family: The Social Organization of Caring as Gendered Work*. Chicago: University of Chicago Press.

Dinnerstein, Dorothy (1976). *The Mermaid and the Minotaur*. New York: Harper & Row.

Dominguez, Joe, and Robin, Vicki (1992). *Your Money or Your Life: Transforming Your Relationship with Money and Achieving Financial Independence*. New York: Viking Penguin.

Donovan, Josephine (1997). *Feminist Theory: The Intellectual Traditions of American Feminism*. New York: Continuum.

Elgin, Duane (1993). *Voluntary Simplicity: Toward a Way of Life That Is Outwardly Simple, Inwardly Rich* (2nd ed.). New York: William Morrow.

Epstein, Barbara (1981). *The Politics of Domesticity: Women, Evangelism, and Temperance in Nineteenth-century America*. Middletown, Conn.: Wesleyan University Press.

———— (1990). "Rethinking Social Movement Theory." *Socialist Review*, 1, 35–65.

Firestone, Shulamith (1979). *The Dialectic of Sex*. London: Woman's Press.

Fitzpatrick, Catherine (1997). "Season Openers: Styles for Spring and Summer Are Over the Field." *Milwaukee Journal Sentinel*, July 23.

Flexner, Eleanor (1975). *Century of Struggle: The Women's Rights Movement in the United States*. Cambridge, Mass.: Belknap Press.

Foucault, Michel (1995). *Discipline and Punish: The Birth of a Prison*. New York: Vintage Books.

Freeman, Jo (1979). "The Women's Liberation Movement: Its Origins, Organizations, Activities and Ideas." In Jo Freeman (ed.), *Women: A Feminist Perspective* (pp. 557–74). Palo Alto, Calif.: Mayfield.

Friedan, Betty (1963). *The Feminine Mystique*. New York: Dell.

———— (1981). *The Second Stage*. New York: Summit Books.

Fulghum, Robert (1986). *All I Really Needed to Know I Learned in Kindergarten: Uncommon Thoughts on Common Things*. New York: Ivy Books.

Gabay, Mary, and Wolfe, Sidney M. (1994). *Unnecessary Cesarean Sections: Curing a National Epidemic*. Washington, D.C: Public Citizen Publications.

Gaskin, Ina May (1977). *Spiritual Midwifery*. Summertown, Tenn.: Book Publishing Co.

Gatto, John (1992). *Dumbing Us Down: The Hidden Curriculum of Compulsory Schooling*. Philadelphia: New Society.

Gerson, Kathleen (1986). *Hard Choices*. Berkeley: University of California Press.

Gerth, H. H., and Mills, C. W. (1946). *From Max Weber: Essays in Sociology*. New York: Oxford University Press.

Gilder, George (1975). *Sexual Suicide*. New York: Bantam.

Gilligan, Carol (1982). *In a Different Voice: Psychological Theory and Women's Development*. Cambridge: Harvard University Press.

Ginsberg, Fay (1989). *Contested Lives: The Abortion Debate in an American Community*. Berkeley: University of California Press.

Glaser, Barney, and Strauss, Anselm (1967). *The Discovery of Grounded Theory: Strategies for Qualitative Research*. Chicago: Aldine.

Glenn, Evelyn Nakano (1991). "Racial Ethnic Women's Labor." In Rae Lesser Blumberg (ed.), *Gender, Family and Economy: The Triple Overlap* (pp. 173–201). Newbury Park, Calif.: Sage.

———— (1994). "Social Constructions of Mothering: A Thematic Overview." In Evelyn Nakano Glenn, Grace Chang, and Linda Rennie Forcey (eds.), *Mothering: Ideology, Experience and Agency* (pp. 1–29). New York: Routledge.

Goldberg, Steven (1973). *The Inevitability of Patriarchy.* New York: William Morrow.

Gordon, Linda (1977). *Woman's Body, Women's Right: A Social History of Birth Control in America.* New York: Penguin Books.

Grant, Judith (1993). *Fundamental Feminism: Contesting the Core Concepts of Feminist Theory.* New York: Routledge.

Grosz, Elizabeth (1990). "Inscription and Body-maps: Representations and the Corporeal." In T. Threadgold and A. Cranny-Francis (eds.), *Feminine/Masculine Representation* (pp. 62–74). Sydney: Allen and Unwin.

Guidera, Mark (1995). "More Americans Ditch the Upscale Life for Emphasis on Family, Environment." *Baltimore Sun,* July 27.

Gusfield, Joseph (1986). *Symbolic Crusade: Status Politics and the American Temperance Movement* (2nd ed.). Champaign: University of Illinois Press.

Hartmann, Heidi (1976). "The Historical Roots of Occupational Segregation: Capitalism, Patriarchy, and Job Segregation by Sex." *Signs,* 1, 137–69.

Hays, Sharon (1996). *The Cultural Contradictions of Motherhood.* New Haven: Yale University Press.

Heckler-Feltz, Cheryl. (1997). "Home Sweet School." *Ohio Magazine,* September, pp. 66–71.

Heilbrun, Catherine (1973). *Toward a Recognition of Androgyny.* New York: Harper Colophon.

Herr, E. L., and Cramer, S. H. (1984). *Career Guidance and Counseling Through the Life Span* (2nd ed.). Boston: Little, Brown.

Hochschild, Arlie (1989). *The Second Shift.* New York: Avon.

Holt, John (1967). *How Children Learn.* New York: Pitman.

––––––– (1989). *Teach Your Own: A Hopeful Path for Education.* New York: Delacorte Press.

hooks, bell (1984). *Feminist Theory: From Margin to Center.* Boston: South End Press.

Husserl, Edmund (1931). *Ideas.* New York: Humanities Press.

Jary, David, and Jary, Julia (1991). *The Harper Collins Dictionary of Sociology.* New York: Harper Collins.

Jenkins, Mercilee (1982). "The Story Is in the Telling: A Cooperative Style of Conversation Among Women." Report No. CS504510. East Lansing, Mich.: National Center for Research on Teacher Learning (ERIC Document Reproduction Service No. ED 238083).

Johnston, Hank, Larana, Enrique, and Gusfield, Joseph (1994). *The New Social Movements.* Philadelphia: Temple University Press.

Jonasdottir, Anne (1988). "On the Concept of Interest: Women's Interests and the Limitations of Interest Theory." In Kathleen Jones and Anne

Jonasdottir (eds.), *The Political Interests of Gender: Developing Theory and Research with a Feminist Face* (pp. 33–65). London: Sage.

Kanter, Rosabeth Moss (1977). *Men and Women of the Corporation.* New York: Basic Books.

Kantrowitz, Barbara, and Wingert, Pat (1998). "Learning at Home: Does It Pass the Test?" *Time,* October 19, pp. 64–71.

Katz Rothman, Barbara (1984). *Giving Birth: Alternatives in Childbirth.* Harrisonburg, Va.: Penguin Books.

——— (1989). *Recreating Motherhood: Ideology and Technology in a Patriarchal Society.* New York: Norton.

——— (1996). "Trends in Midwifery: The Dutch Example." Lecture delivered at the Seattle Midwifery School, Seattle, February.

Kasper, Anne (1994). "A Feminist, Qualitative Methodology: A Study of Women with Breast Cancer." *Qualitative Sociology,* 17, 263–81.

Kaufmann, Debra (1991). *Rachel's Daughters.* New Brunswick, N.J.: Rutgers University Press.

Kehoe, Colleen, and Pitkow, James (1996). "Emerging Trends in the WWW User Population." *Communications of the ACM,* 39, 6.

Kessler, Suzanne J., and McKenna, Wendy (1978). *Gender: An Ethnomethodological Approach.* New York: John Wiley.

Kitzinger, Sheila (1992). *Breastfeeding Your Baby.* New York: Alfred A. Knopf.

Klandermans, Bert, and Tarrow, Sidney (1988). "Mobilization Into Social Movements: Synthesizing European and American Approaches." In *International Social Movement Research* (pp. 1–38). Greenwich, Conn.: JAI Press.

Knight-Ridder News Service (1996). "Feeling Tired? Feeling Stressed?" *Janesville Gazette,* February 22.

Korhauser, William (1959). *The Politics of Mass Society.* Glencoe, Ill.: Free Press.

Koven, Seth, and Michel, Sonya (1993). Introduction: "Mother Worlds." In Seth Koven and Sonya Michel (eds.), *Mothers of a New World: Maternalist Politics and the Origins of Welfare States* (pp. 1–42). New York: Routledge.

Ladd-Taylor, Molly (1993). "Mothers and the Making of the Sheppard-Towner Act." In Seth Koven and Sonya Michel (eds.), *Mothers of a New World: Maternalist Politics and the Origins of Welfare States* (pp. 321–42). New York: Routledge.

La Leche League International (1958). *The Womanly Art of Breastfeeding.* Franklin Park, Ill.: La Leche League.

——— (1987). *The Womanly Art of Breastfeeding* (6th ed.). Franklin Park, Ill: La Leche League

Langellier, Kristin, and Peterson, Eric (1984). "Spinstorying: A Communication Analysis of Women's Storytelling." Paper presented at the Speech Communication Association Convention, Chicago, November.

Lanigan, Richard (1988). *Phenomenology of Communication: Merleau-Ponty's Thematics in Communicology and Semiology.* Pittsburgh, Pa.: Duquesne University Press.

Lawrence, Ruth (1994). *Breastfeeding: A Guide for the Medical Profession* (4th ed.). St. Louis, Mo.: Mosby Year Book.

Liedloff, Jean (1985). *The Continuum Concept.* Reading, Mass.: Addison-Wesley.

Lines, Patricia (1991). "Home Instruction: The Size and Growth of the Movement." In J. Van Galen and M. A. Pitman (eds.), *Home Schooling: Political, Historical and Pedagogical Perspectives* (pp. 9–41). Norwood, N.J.: Ablex.

Lofland, John, and Lofland, Lyn (1984). *Analyzing Social Settings.* Reading, Mass.: Addison-Wesley.

Longacre, Doris (1981). *Living More with Less.* Scottdale, Pa.: Herald Press.

Lorber, Judith (1994). *Paradoxes of Gender.* New Haven: Yale University Press.

Luhrs, Janet (1997). *The Simple Living Guide.* New York: Broadway Books.

Lupton, Deborah (1994). *Medicine as Culture: Illness, Disease, and the Body in Western Societies.* Thousand Oaks, Calif.: Sage.

McAdam, Doug (1982). *Political Process and the Development of Black Insurgency, 1930–1970.* Chicago: University of Chicago Press.

McBride, G. G. (1994). *On Wisconsin Women: Working for Their Rights from Settlement to Suffrage.* Madison: University of Wisconsin Press.

McCarthy, John, and Zald, Mayer (1973). *The Trend of Social Movements in America.* Morristown, N.J.: General Learning Press.

——— (1977). "Resource Mobilization and Social Movements: A Partial Theory." *American Journal of Sociology,* 82, 1212–41.

McIntosh, Peggy (1989). "White Privilege: Unpacking the Invisible Knapsack." *Peace and Freedom,* July/August, pp. 10–12.

Martin, Emily (1987). *The Woman in the Body: A Cultural Analysis of Reproduction.* Boston: Beacon Press.

May, Elaine Tyler (1988). *Homeward Bound: American Families in the Cold War Era.* New York: Basic Books.

Melucci, Alberto (1985). "The Symbolic Challenge of Contemporary Movements." *Social Research,* 52, 789–815.

———. (1989). *Nomads of the Present.* London: Hutchinson Radius.

Mendolsohn, Robert (1984). *How to Raise a Healthy Child in Spite of Your Doctor.* New York: Ballantine Books.

Michel, Sonya (1993). "The Limits of Maternalism: Policies Toward American Wage-earning Mothers During the Progressive Era." In Seth

Koven and Sonya Michel (eds.), *Mothers of a New World: Maternalist Politics and the Origins of Welfare States* (pp. 277–320). New York: Routledge.

Mies, Maria (1988). *Patriarchy and Accumulation on a World Scale: Women in the International Division of Labor.* Atlantic Highlands, N.J.: Zed Books.

Milkman, Ruth (1979). "Women's Work and the Economic Crisis: Some Lessons from the Great Depression." In Nancy Cott and Elizabeth Pleck (eds.), *A Heritage of Her Own: Toward a New Social History of American Women* (pp. 507–41). New York: Simon and Schuster.

———. (1989). "Rosie the Riveter Revisited: Management's Postwar Purge of Women Automobile Workers." In Nelson Lichtenstein and Stephen Meyer (eds.), *On the Line* (pp. 129–52). Chicago: University of Chicago Press.

Morris, Aldon (1984). *The Origins of the Civil Rights Movement.* New York: Free Press.

Morris, Desmond (1969). *The Naked Ape.* St. Albans: Panther.

Mothering (1994). "Our Readers Make Choices" (brochure). Santa Fe, N.M.: Author.

Mothering (1995–96). Bimonthly magazine.

Nearing, Scott, and Nearing, Helen (1990). *The Good Life: Helen and Scott Nearing's Sixty Years of Self-Sufficient Living.* New York: Schocken Books.

Nesbit, R. C. (1989). *Wisconsin: A History* (2nd ed.). Updated by William F. Thompson. Madison: University of Wisconsin Press.

Nolen, T. P. (1994). "Choosing Voluntary Simplicity as a Lifestyle." *Dissertation Abstracts International,* 55 (09B). No. AAG9502689.

Nye, David (1996). "Fibromyalgia—A Guide for Patients." http://www.sunflower.org/~cfsdays/nye.htm.

O'Connor, Bonnie (1993). "The Home Birth Movement in the United States." *Journal of Medicine and Philosophy,* 18, 147–74.

O'Mara, Peggy (1991). *The Way Back Home: Essays on Life and Family.* Santa Fe, N.M.: Mothering Publications.

O'Neill, Jessie (1997). *The Golden Ghetto: The Psychology of Affluence.* Milwaukee: Affluenza Project.

Pearce, J. C. (1977). *Magical Child.* New York: Dutton.

Pierce, L. B. (1999). *Choosing Simplicity: Real People Finding Fulfillment in a Complex World.* Carmel, Calif.: Gallagher Press.

Piven, Frances Fox, and Cloward, Richard (1977). *Poor People's Movements: Why They Succeed, How They Fail.* New York: Pantheon.

Ray, B. D. (1996). "Research Report." *Court Report,* April, pp. 1–3.

Reskin, Barbara, and Padavic, Irene (1994). *Women and Men at Work.* Thousand Oaks, Calif.: Pine Forge Press.

Rich, Adrienne (1977). *Of Woman Born: Motherhood as Experience and Institution.* New York: Bantam.

Rossiter, M. W. (1982). *Women Scientists in America: Struggles and Strategies to 1940*. Baltimore: Johns Hopkins Press.

Ruddick, Sara (1983). "Maternal Thinking." In Joyce Treblicot (ed.), *Mothering: Essays in Feminist Theory* (pp. 213–30). Totowa, N.J.: Rowman and Allanheld.

Ryan, A. S. (1997). "The Resurgence of Breastfeeding in the US." *Pediatrics*, 99 (4), 12e.

Ryan, Mary P. (1981). *The Cradle of the Middle Class: The Family in Oneida County, N.Y., 1790–1865*. Cambridge: Cambridge University Press.

——— (1983). *Womanhood in America: From Colonial Times to the Present* (3rd ed.). New York: Franklin Watts.

St. James, Elaine (1994). *Simplify Your Life: 100 Ways to Slow Down and Enjoy the Things That Really Matter*. New York: Hyperion.

——— (1995). *Inner Simplicity: 100 Ways to Regain Peace and Nourish Your Soul*. New York: Hyperion.

——— (1996). *Living the Simple Life: A Guide to Scaling Down and Enjoying More*. New York: Hyperion.

St. James, Elaine, and Cole, Vera (2000). *Simplify Your Life with Kids*. New York: Hyperion.

Schor, Juliet (1992). *The Overworked American: The Unexpected Decline of Leisure*. New York: Basic.

——— (1995). "Why (and How) More People Are Dropping Out of the Rat Race." *Working Woman*, August, p. 14.

——— (1998). *The Overspent American: Upscaling, Downshifting and the New Consumer*. New York: Basic.

Schor, Naomi, and Weed, Elizabeth (eds.) (1994). *The Essential Difference*. Bloomington: Indiana University Press.

Sears, William, and Sears, Martha (1993). *The Baby Book*. New York: Little, Brown.

Shama, Avraham (1988). "The Voluntary Simplicity Consumer: A Comparative Study." *Psychological Reports*, 63, 859–69.

Shama, Avraham, and Wisenblit, Joseph (1984). "Values of Voluntary Simplicity: Lifestyle and Motivation." *Psychological Reports*, 55, 231–40.

Shi, David (1985). *The Simple Life: Plain Living and High Thinking in American Culture*. New York: Oxford University Press.

Simple Living Network (1997). http://www.slnet.com.

Sklar, Kathryn Kish (1993). "The Historical Foundations of Women's Power in the Creation of the American Welfare State, 1830–1930." In Seth Koven and Sonya Michel (eds.), *Mothers of a New World: Maternalist Politics and the Origins of Welfare States* (pp. 43–93). New York: Routledge.

Skocpol, Theda (1992). *Protecting Soldiers and Mothers: The Political Origins of Social Policy in the United States*. Cambridge, Mass.: Belknap Press.

Smelser, Neil (1962). *Theory of Collective Behavior.* New York: Free Press.

Smith, Dorothy (1987). *The Everyday World as Problematic: A Feminist Sociology.* Toronto: University of Toronto Press.

Smith-Rosenberg, Carroll. (1979). "The Beauty, the Beast and the Militant Woman: A Case Study in Sex Roles and Social Stress in Jacksonian America." In Nancy Cott and Elizabeth Pleck (eds.), *A Heritage of Her Own: Toward a New Social History of American Women* (pp. 197–221). New York: Simon and Schuster.

Spirn, Anne W. (1995). "Constructing Nature: The Legacy of Frederick Law Olmstead." In William Cronon (ed.), *Uncommon Ground: Toward Reinventing Nature* (pp. 91–113). New York: W. W. Norton.

Strauss, Anselm, and Corbin, Juliet (1990). *Basics of Qualitative Research: Grounded Theory, Procedures and Techniques.* Newbury Park, Calif.: Sage.

Sullivan, Deborah A., and Weitz, Rose (1988). *Labor Pains: Modern Midwives and Homebirth.* New Haven and London: Yale University Press.

Sullivan, Richard (1995). "Linking Labor and New Social Movements: The P-9 Example." Manuscript.

Taylor, Steven, and Bogdan, Robert (1984). *Introduction to Qualitative Research Methods: The Search for Meanings.* New York: John Wiley & Sons.

Taylor, Verta (1996). *Rock-a-by Baby: Feminism, Self-help and Postpartum Depression.* New York: Routledge.

Taylor, Verta, and Whittier, Nancy (1992). "Collective Identity in Social Movement Communities: Lesbian Feminist Mobilization." In Aldon Morris and Carol M. Mueller (eds.), *Frontiers in Social Movement Theory* (pp. 104–29). New Haven: Yale University Press.

——— (1995). "Analytical Approaches to Social Movement Culture: The Culture of the Women's Movement." In Hank Johnston and Bert Klandermans (eds.), *Social Movements and Culture* (pp. 163–87). Minneapolis: University of Minnesota Press.

Thevenin, Tine (1976). *The Family Bed.* Minneapolis: Thevenin.

Thurer, Shari (1994). *The Myths of Motherhood: How Culture Reinvents the Good Mother.* New York: Penguin Books.

Tiger, Lionel (1969). *Men in Groups.* London: Nelson.

Tilly, Charles (1978). *From Mobilization to Revolution.* Reading, Mass.: Addison-Wesley.

Touraine, Alain (1985). "An Introduction to the Study of Social Movements." *Social Research,* 52, 4.

Treblicot, Joyce (ed.) (1983). *Mothering: Essays in Feminist Theory.* Totowa, N.J.: Rowman and Allanheld.

TV-Free America (1998). "Television Statistics" (brochure). Washington, D.C.: Author.

Umanksy, Lauri. (1996). *Motherhood Reconceived: Feminism and the Legacies of the Sixties*. New York and London: New York University Press.

Van Maanen, John (1988). *Tales of the Field: On Writing Ethnography*. Chicago: University of Chicago Press.

Waldorf Education (1999). Steiner College, November 1. http://www.steinercollege.org/waldorf.htm.

Welter, Barbara (1976). *Dimity Convictions: The American Woman in the Nineteenth Century*. Athens: Ohio University Press.

West, Candace, and Zimmerman, Donald (1987). "Doing Gender." *Gender & Society*, 1, 13–37.

Whalen, Jack, and Flacks, Richard (1984). "Echoes of Rebellion: The Liberated Generation Grows Up." *Journal of Political and Military Sociology*, 12, 61–78.

Wilson, Elizabeth (1991). *The Sphinx in the City: Urban Life, the Control of Disorder and Women*. Berkeley: University of California Press.

Young, Iris (1990). *Throwing Like a Girl and Other Essays in Feminist Philosophy and Social Theory*. Bloomington: University of Indiana Press.

Zelitzer, Vivian (1985). *Pricing the Priceless Child: The Changing Social Value of Children*. New York: Basic Books.

175. BOBEL: NM is yet another accomodation to male privilege

175: BOBEl on ethics of her study on NM.

179. BOBEl did not share her intentions of the NM she used in her study.

184. BOBEl belives lack of cultural diversity is a key characteristic of NM.

185. _Helpful info for conducting research_

186. create a loose set of criteria.

read From 185 - 198 to hear about how the research was conducted.

Index

The letter *t* after a page number indicates a table; *f* indicates a figure.

QUESTion for school kids:

Do you enjoy Being @ home or @ school MORE?

why?
Do you have a BETTER re   up w/
your family or school?

Bobel says that ~~parents~~ NATural/mothers claim to "just know", To "feel" to Be "in tune w/ their instincts y intuition", But, says Bobel,

p62. issues BoBel says have not Been addressed regarding the quality effects y Natural mothering.